Workshop on Discontinuous Structures in Natural Language Processing (DiscoNLP 2016)

Held at the 2016 Conference of the North American Chapter of the Association for Computational Linguistics: Human Language Technologies (NAACL HLT 2016)

San Diego, California, USA
17 June 2016

ISBN: 978-1-5108-2521-5

NAACL HLT 2016

**Workshop on Discontinuous Structures
in Natural Language Processing (DiscoNLP)**

Proceedings of the Workshop

June 17, 2016
San Diego, California, USA

Introduction

This volume presents the papers presented at the Workshop on Discontinuous Structures in Natural Language Processing, held in San Diego, California on June 17, 2016 during the 15th Annual Conference of the North American Chapter of the Association for Computational Linguistics: Human Language Technologies.

The modeling of certain structures in natural language requires a mechanism for discontinuity, in the sense that we must account for two or more parts of the structure that are not adjacent. This is true across many languages and on different description levels. For instance, on the lexical level, this concerns discontinuous morphological phenomena such as transfixation (templatic morphology), as well as phrasal verbs, and non-contiguous multiword expressions. On the syntactic level, discontinuity is caused by phenomena such as extraposition and topicalization, or argument scrambling. Morphologically rich languages (MRLs) are particularly likely to exhibit such phenomena. Other examples include disfluency and anaphora/coreference resolution with discontinuous antecedents; modeling in both of the latter areas requires an extended domain of locality. On a higher level, discontinuity is a relevant factor in machine translation, as well as in complex question answering and in topic structure modeling. Discontinuity has been studied intensively in a range of different areas, including but not limited to grammar development, syntactic and semantic parsing, morphological analysis, machine translation, anaphora resolution, discourse modeling, automatic summarization and complex question answering.

Nevertheless, the treatment of discontinuous structures remains a challenge, because on the one hand, recovering of non-local information is generally associated with a high computational cost, and on the other hand, discontinuities are inherently a low-frequency phenomenon, which means that statistical approaches have a tendency to analyze them incorrectly as more frequent local phenomena. Additionally, it is not always clear if and how NLP tasks can benefit from knowing about discontinuity, that is, why one should care, particularly considering the given computational cost. The goal of this workshop is to bring together researchers from the different areas to give them a forum to exchange ideas and problem solutions, to create synergy effects, and to enable more powerful solutions. This encompasses not only linguistic analyses and work on analyzing or recovering the corresponding structures, such as, e.g., in non-projective dependency parsing, but also studies on "use cases", which show how information about discontinuity can be used to enhance NLP tasks. We think that given the broad program we have put together, this goal has been more than fulfilled.

Thanks to all authors who have contributed their work! Out of ten submissions, seven were selected for presentation. We would also like to extend our gratitude the program committee, who have dedicated their time and effort in order to make this workshop a high-quality event.

See you in San Diego!

Wolfgang Maier, Sandra Kübler, and Constantin Orăsan

Organizers:

Wolfgang Maier, University of Düsseldorf (Germany)
Sandra Kübler, Indiana University (USA)
Constantin Orăsan, University of Wolverhampton (UK)

Program Committee:

Anne Abeillé, University Paris 7 (France)
Krasimir Angelov, University of Gothenburg (Sweden)
Marianna Apidianaki, LIMSI (France)
Eric de la Clergerie, INRIA (France)
Andreas van Cranenburgh, Royal Netherlands Academy for Arts and Sciences (The Netherlands)
Joachim Daiber, University of Amsterdam (The Netherlands)
Carlos Gómez Rodríguez, University of A Coruña (Spain)
Eva Hasler, University of Cambridge (UK)
Mijail Kabadjov, University of Essex (UK)
Sylvain Kahane, University Paris 10 (France)
Laura Kallmeyer, University of Düsseldorf (Germany)
Philipp Koehn, University of Edinburgh (UK)
Johannes Leveling, Elsevier (The Netherlands)
Timm Lichte, University of Düsseldorf (Germany)
Peter Ljunglöf, University of Gothenburg (Sweden)
Georgiana Marsic, University of Wolverhampton (UK)
Detmar Meurers, University of Tübingen (Germany)
Jean-Luc Minel, Université Paris Ouest Nanterre La Défense (France)
Sara Moze, University of Wolverhampton (UK)
Philippe Muller, University of Toulouse/IRIT (France)
Preslav Nakov, Qatar Computing Research Institute (Qatar)
Mark-Jan Nederhof, University of St. Andrews (UK)
Yannick Parmentier, University of Orléans (France)
Ted Pedersen, University of Minnesota (USA)
Irene Renau, Pontificia Universidad Católica de Valparaíso (Chile)
Lonneke van der Plas, University of Malta (Malta)
Natalie Schluter, University of Copenhagen (Denmark)
Djamé Seddah, University Paris 4 (France)
Khalil Sima'an, University of Amsterdam (The Netherlands)
Yannick Versley, University of Heidelberg (Germany)
Suzan Veberne, University of Nijmegen (The Netherlands)
Andy Way, Dublin City University (Ireland)

Invited Speaker:

David Chiang, University of Notre Dame (USA)

Table of Contents

An LFG Account of Discontinuous Nominal Expressions
Liselotte Snijders 1

Non-projectivity and valency
Zdenka Uresova, Eva Fucikova and Jan Hajic 12

Machine Translation of Non-Contiguous Multiword Units
Anabela Barreiro and Fernando Batista 22

Discontinuous VP in Bulgarian
Elisaveta Balabanova 31

Discontinuous Genitives in Hindi/Urdu
Sebastian Sulger 37

Discontinuous parsing with continuous trees
Wolfgang Maier and Timm Lichte 47

Discontinuity Re^2-visited: A Minimalist Approach to Pseudoprojective Constituent Parsing
Yannick Versley 58

Workshop Program

Friday, June 17, 2016

9:30–10:00   *An LFG Account of Discontinuous Nominal Expressions*
Liselotte Snijders

10:00–10:30   *Non-projectivity and valency*
Zdenka Uresova, Eva Fucikova and Jan Hajic

10:30–11:00   *Coffee break*

11:00–12:15   *Invited Talk: Finite automata for free word order languages*
David Chiang

12:15–12:45   *Machine Translation of Non-Contiguous Multiword Units*
Anabela Barreiro and Fernando Batista

12:45–14:30   *Lunch break*

2:30–3:00   *Discontinuous VP in Bulgarian*
Elisaveta Balabanova

3:00–3:30   *Discontinuous Genitives in Hindi/Urdu*
Sebastian Sulger

4:00–4:30   *Discontinuous parsing with continuous trees*
Wolfgang Maier and Timm Lichte

4:30–5:00   *Discontinuity Re^2-visited: A Minimalist Approach to Pseudoprojective Constituent Parsing*
Yannick Versley

5:00–5:45   *Panel discussion*

An LFG Account of Discontinuous Nominal Expressions

Liselotte Snijders
Waseda University
Tokyo, Japan
liselottesnijders@gmail.com

Abstract

This paper presents an overview of an LFG treatment of discontinuous nominal expressions involving modification, making the claim that cross-linguistically different types of discontinuity (i.e. in Warlpiri and English) should be captured by the same overall analysis, despite being licensed in different ways. LFG's separation of grammatical functions from phrase structural positions intuitively accounts for discontinuous expressions, and its use of glue semantics ensures that discontinuous and contiguous expressions receive the same semantic analysis.

1 Introduction

Discontinuity of nominal expressions, a phenomenon in which two or more parts of a semantic nominal unit are non-adjacent in phrase structure, is prevalent in languages traditionally classified as "non-configurational" (Hale, 1983), e.g. the Australian languages Warlpiri, Wambaya, Jaminjung (Simpson, 1991; Nordlinger, 1998; Schultze-Berndt and Simard, 2012), Latin (Devine and Stephens, 2000; Spevak, 2010), Ancient Greek (Devine and Stephens, 2006), and are also attested in a number of Slavic languages, e.g. Russian (Sekerina, 1997; Sekerina, 1999) and Polish (Siewierska, 1984). An example of nominal discontinuity from Warlpiri is shown in (1) (Simpson, 1991, p. 282):[1]

[1]This type of Warlpiri example has another interpretation, which can be translated as 'The child$_i$ is chasing it and it$_i$ is small' (Simpson, 1991). Based on Simpson's work this appears to be secondary predication rather than discontinuity, therefore I only take the interpretation in (1) into account.

(1) ***Kurdu-ngku*** *ka* *wajilipi-nyi*
     child-ERG   PRES chase-NONPAST
     wita-ngku
     small-ERG
     'The small child is chasing it.'

In (1) a head noun is separated from a modifier, but both parts map to the same grammatical function (subject). The two parts of the discontinuous expression share the same case-marking. A similar type of discontinuity involving modification is attested in English, in the cases of relative clause extraposition in (2a) and NP-PP split in (2b) (Kirkwood, 1977, p. 55):[2]

(2) a. **The man** entered **who I met yesterday.**

    b. **A number of stories** soon appeared **about Watergate**.

A similar type of discontinuity is in fact also attested in Warlpiri (Hale, 1976, p. 78):[3]

(3) *Ngajulu-rlu* *rna* ***yankirri*** *pantu-rnu*
     I-ERG   AUX emu.ABS spear-PAST
     kuja-lpa ***ngapa*** ***nga-rnu***.
     COMP-AUX water.ABS drink-PAST
     'I speared the emu that was drinking water.'

[2]Another type of discontinuity in English involving modification is partial fronting, e.g. **About Japan**, *the woman wrote many books*; additional examples are discussed in Section 6.

[3]Hale (1976) refers to this type of example as 'adjoined relative clause': it can also precede the sentence as a whole (somewhat like a hanging topic). It can also have a temporal reading: 'I speared the emu while it was drinking water'.

1

Proceedings of DiscoNLP 2016, pages 1–11,
San Diego, California, June 17, 2016. ©2016 Association for Computational Linguistics

Discontinuity of nominal expressions, whether of the kind in which two words are marked with the same case (as in (1)), or of the kind in which a modifier of an argument is postposed to follow the clause (as in (2) and (3)) presents a challenge for syntactic theory, as it requires the two or more parts of syntactic information to be united in the semantics.

In this paper I illustrate how discontinuous nominal expressions can be accounted for within the Lexical-Functional Grammar (LFG) framework based on previous work. With its constraint-based nature and parallel architecture, LFG provides a straightforward way of handling discontinuity by allowing two or more separate parts of phrase structural information to map to the same functional structure, and thereby to the same semantic structure. The focus of this paper is on nominal discontinuity involving modification specifically (i.e. a head and a modifier being separated), to limit the scope of discussion, but Section 8 briefly addresses a different type of discontinuity in comparison. I make the claim that discontinuous nominal expressions (involving modification) in typologically different languages (i.e. in Warlpiri and English) are instances of the same phenomenon and therefore require the same analysis, despite being licensed by somewhat different phrase structure rules. I propose a definition that captures both types of discontinuity, and illustrate that LFG is capable of accounting for the different types in a straightforward fashion.

Overall I aim to illustrate LFG's potential in contributing to a potential implementation of discontinuity in NLP systems, because of its straightforward account of discontinuity, not requiring any special mechanisms. Discontinuous data is more challenging for approaches which parse sentences based on linear ordering, such as dependency grammar and approaches relying on surface phrase structure configuration. LFG is computationally implementable and has been implemented in the XLE system (Crouch et al., 2011). This paper thereby contributes to potential enhancements of NLP tasks with regards to discontinuity.

2 Lexical-Functional Grammar

Lexical-Functional Grammar (LFG) (Kaplan and Bresnan, 1982) is a constraint-based syntactic framework which posits a parallel architecture, separating information about grammatical functions from phrase structural configuration. For this reason it is well-suited to account for languages with relatively free ordering of grammatical functions (e.g. Warlpiri). LFG posits two syntactic levels: constituent structure (c-structure) and functional structure (f-structure). C-structure encodes information about linear precedence, dominance relations and constituency, and is represented as a phrase structure tree. F-structure hosts information about the grammatical functions of the predicate of a sentence (including adjuncts), along with a range of morphosyntactic information such as case, number, tense and aspect. It is represented as an attribute-value matrix. C-structure nodes are locally annotated with information about grammatical functions and/or lexical information. Each c-structure node is associated with a particular f-structure, and a local annotation on the c-structure node ensures the mapping of the c-structure node to this f-structure via the ϕ function. Specifically, the local annotation on a particular c-structure node specifies the relation of the f-structure associated with this node to the f-structure associated with its mother node. An example of this mapping for the simple sentence *John walked* is shown in Figure 1.

In the annotations on c-structure, $\uparrow$ points to the f-structure of the mother node and $\downarrow$ points to the f-structure of the current node. The annotation $\uparrow = \downarrow$ thus expresses that the f-structure of the mother node is the same as the f-structure of its daughter node, and the annotation $(\uparrow \text{SUBJ}) = \downarrow$ expresses that the daughter node maps to the subject of its mother's f-structure. In English, this subject annotation is structurally associated with the NP node that is in the specifier of IP position (see Section 5). The grammatical functions SUBJ and OBJ (as well as a number of other functions assumed in LFG, such as OBJ_θ and OBL_θ) are unique, e.g. a verb can only have one subject which it subcategorizes for. This subcategorization is marked in the lexical annotation on *walked* in Figure 1, $(\uparrow \text{PRED}) = $ 'walk$<$SUBJ$>$', which states that the predicate (PRED) value of this word is 'walk' and takes one argument, SUBJ. Adjuncts (ADJ) are not unique, but map to a set, by means of the annotation $\downarrow \in (\uparrow \text{ADJ})$, to be discussed in more detail in the next section.

3 Discontinuity in LFG

3.1 Previous Work

Discontinuous nominal expressions have been analyzed in LFG by Simpson (1991) (Warlpiri), Kuhn (1999; 2001) (German), Cavar and Seiss (2011) (New-Shtokavian) and are discussed by Snijders (2012; 2015).[4] Simpson (1991) and Kuhn (1999; 2001) share a similar overall analysis in assuming that two parts of a discontinuous nominal expression map to the same f-structure. Here I focus on Simpson's (1991) analysis. Simpson's analysis for example (1), adapted to fit with her more recently proposed c-structure for Warlpiri (Simpson, 2007), is shown in Figure 2 (leaving out lexical annotations).[5]

Crucially, the two parts of the discontinuous expressions both map to the f-structure of the subject of the predicate. The annotation $\downarrow \in (\uparrow \text{ADJ})$ on the N node states that this node ($\downarrow$) maps to the set of adjuncts of the NP node ($\uparrow$). Note that the object, despite being absent in c-structure, is present in f-structure as the verb requires an object: its PRED value is 'PRO'.

The overall f-structure for the contiguous example is the same, as shown by the annotations on the c-structure of the contiguous version of example (1), shown in Figure 3. Unlike in English, in the Warlpiri c-structures the subject annotation comes from the case-marking, not from the structural position.

The example with the discontinuous expression and the contiguous one thus have the same f-structure, which is mapped to the same semantic structure, as will be discussed in Section 7.

3.2 English Extraposition

Previous work in LFG does not discuss discontinuous nominal expressions in English, nor does it provide an account of how discontinuity in differ-

ent languages is licensed in different ways. One type of English discontinuity, extraposition, will be addressed here, and I show that it requires the same treatment as the discontinuity with two case-marked nominals as found in Warlpiri, providing a cross-linguistic definition of discontinuous nominal expressions in Section 4. I show that any cross-linguistic differences are due to differences in c-structure rules (phrase structure rules).

Discontinuity involving extraposition and discontinuity involving two words with the same case-marking have in common the fact that two parts of the same grammatical functions are not adjacent in phrase structure. In the instance of relative clause extraposition in English, I propose to represent the extraposed clause by means of an adjoined CP clause.[6] The structure I propose for (2a) is shown in Figure 4 with partial annotations. In the case of (2b) we would instead have an adjoined PP.

I note a few differences between the type of discontinuity with two case-marked nominals (Figure 2) and the English extraposition one (Figure 4). Linguistically, a difference is the type of categories that may be separated from each other, i.e. in Warlpiri two nominals, while in English an NP and a CP or PP. A second point of linguistic variation is the position that the two or more parts of the discontinuous expression may appear in. In English this is restricted, shown by the unacceptability of *A number of stories soon about Watergate appeared.* In the case of Warlpiri discontinuity in which the subparts have the same case-marking, the placement of the subparts is much freer, reflecting Warlpiri's property of free placement of grammatical functions.[7]

Another difference between the discontinuous expression in Warlpiri in Figure 2 and the English one in Figure 4 is the type of annotation on the modifier:

---

[4]There is other work on long-distance dependencies in LFG (e.g. Kaplan and Zaenen (1989), Clément et al. (2002) among others), but this literature discusses cases of arguments appearing outside the clause that they are part of (e.g. *wh*-fronting out of embedded clauses). This is a different type of long-distance dependency than the discontinuous nominal expressions discussed here, as the latter case involves two parts of the same grammatical function being separated.

[5]It is generally assumed that adjective-like elements in Warlpiri are of the N category (Hale, 1983; Simpson, 1991; Hale et al., 1995).

[6]The CP does not form a constituent with the VP, as preposing of both is ruled out: *'Entered who I saw yesterday, the man'. For this reason adjunction to IP is appropriate.

[7]However, like word order, discontinuity is not random, but is triggered by information structure, as discussed by De Jong (1986) (Latin), Cavar and Seiss (2011) (New-Shtokavian) and Schultze-Berndt and Simard (2012) (Jaminjung). A full discussion of the information structure of discontinuous expressions is beyond the scope of this paper. Also, recall that Warlpiri does appear to have a type of extraposition as shown in (3), which seems more restricted in its placement than the type of discontinuity involving case-marked nominals.

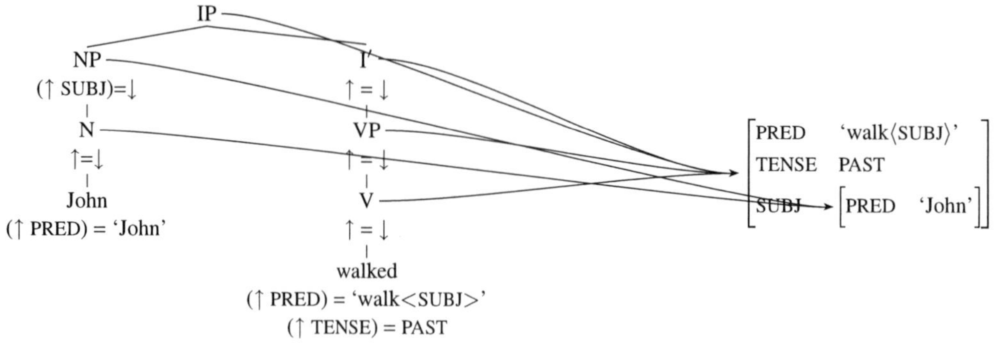

Figure 1: An illustration of c- to f-structure mapping.

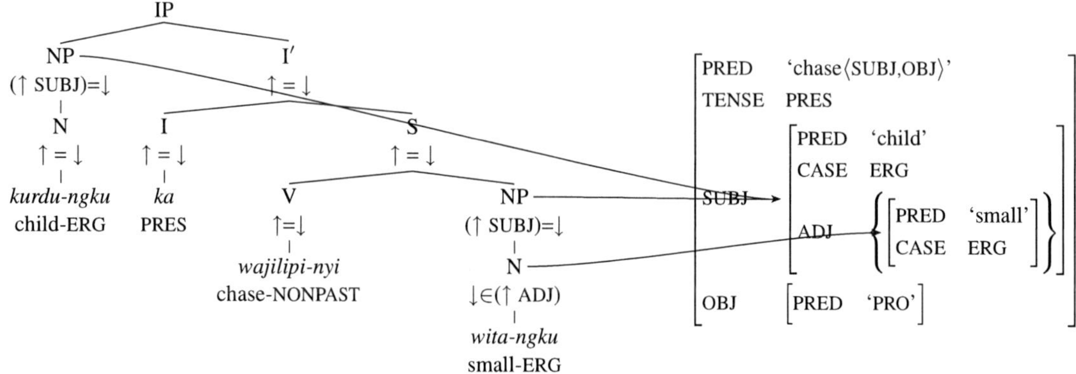

Figure 2: C- to f-structure mapping of a discontinuous expression.

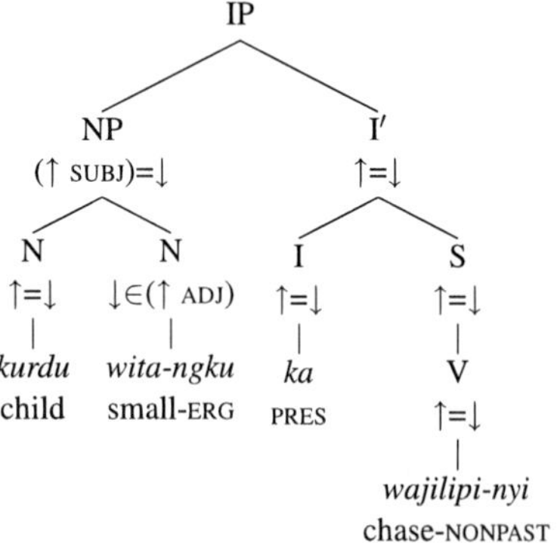

Figure 3: C-structure for a contiguous example, mapping to the f-structure in Figure 2.

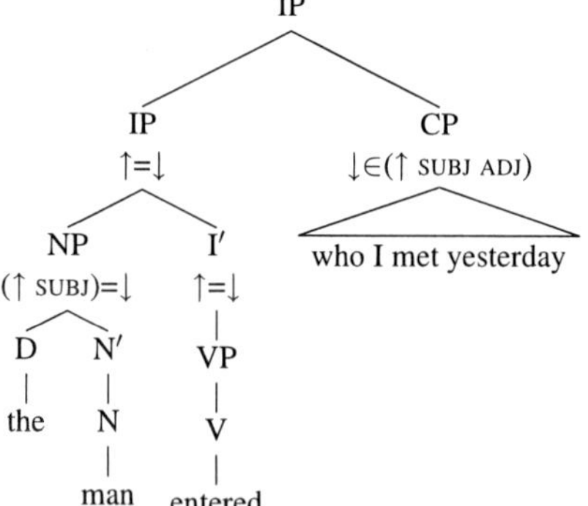

Figure 4: C-structure for English relative clause extraposition.

in the Warlpiri case both head and modifier map to the same f-structure directly (subject of the predicate by means of the annotation (↑ SUBJ) = ↓). In the English case, the modifier maps to the f-structure of the adjunct of the SUBJ, whereas the head maps to the overall f-structure of the SUBJ. The annotations are thus somewhat different, but the end result for both examples is the same: both head and modifier are contained within the f-structure of the subject. This

is an important observation, as we would have the same f-structure mapping even with different annotations. For example, in the Warlpiri c-structure in Figure 2, the annotations on the two NPs are both (↑ SUBJ) = ↓, both mapping to the same f-structure, but we could also imagine a set of annotations where the adjunct has the annotation ↓∈ (↑ SUBJ ADJ). A definition of discontinuity needs to abstract away from this variation in annotation, which is reflected in the definition proposed in the following section.

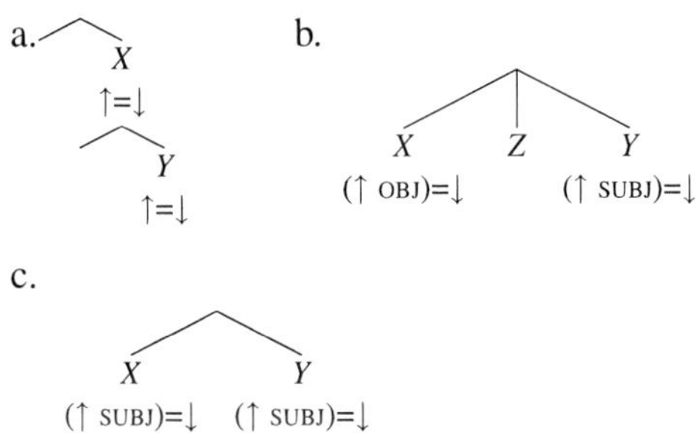

a. / b. / c.

(↑ OBJ)=↓   (↑ SUBJ)=↓

(↑ SUBJ)=↓   (↑ SUBJ)=↓

Figure 5: Structures not fulfilling the conditions of definition (4).

4 Definition of Discontinuity in LFG

In order to capture nominal discontinuity in a more formal way, I propose the following definition:[8]

(4) **Nominal discontinuous expressions:**
Given two c-structure constituents X and Y, $X \neq Y$, $\{X, Y\}$ form a discontinuous nominal expression iff:

   i. Neither X nor Y dominate the other; and

   ii. X and Y map to the f-structure or sub-f-structure of the same grammatical function; and

   iii. The yield of X is not string adjacent to the yield of Y; and

   iv. The constituent(s) that intervene(s) between X and Y do(es) not map to the f-structure or any sub-f-structure of the grammatical function that X and Y map to.

The key here is that the two parts of a discontinuous expression both map to the f-structure of the same grammatical function, or to an f-structure that is contained within the f-structure of this grammatical function. Consider the partial structures shown in Figure 5, all of which do not fulfill all conditions of definition (4).

Condition (i) rules out structure (a) in Figure 5 as being discontinuous; X and Y here map to the same f-structure, but X dominates Y. Condition (ii) rules

---

[8]One reviewer points out that these conditions (especially (i), (iii) and (iv)) do not confine to nominals. However, this paper restricts itself to nominal expressions (involving modification); extending the definition to other kinds of discontinuity is briefly addressed in Section 8.

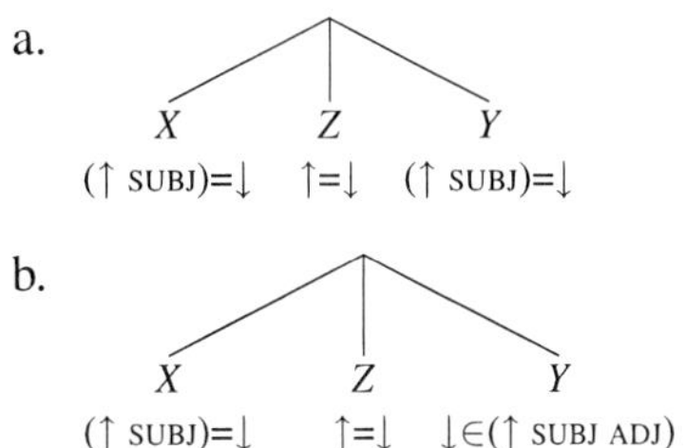

a.

(↑ SUBJ)=↓   ↑=↓   (↑ SUBJ)=↓

b.

(↑ SUBJ)=↓   ↑=↓   ↓∈(↑ SUBJ ADJ)

Figure 6: Instances of discontinuous nominal expressions.

out the structure in Figure 5 (b) as an instance of discontinuity. In this structure the yield of X is not string adjacent to the yield of Y (in other words, the edges of X and Y do not coincide), but X and Y do not map to the f-structure (or sub-f-structure) of the same grammatical function. Condition (iii) ensures that there is an intervening element, and rules out the structure in Figure 5 (c) as an instance of discontinuity.

The structure in Figure 6 (a) fulfills all conditions as listed in (4), including condition (iv). Finally, according to condition (ii) in (4), the structure in Figure 6 (b) is also a case of discontinuity.

5 Constraining Discontinuity

The definition of nominal discontinuity in (4) covers both the type of nominal discontinuity attested with two case-marked nominals (one of which modifies the other) and the type with an extraposed modifier clause. Their analysis is very similar in terms of their c- to f-structure mapping, but the way in which the two different types are licensed is somewhat different. The case-marked nominal type of discontinuity is made possible by the assumption in LFG that in languages like Warlpiri grammatical functions are assigned lexically and not by phrase structure configuration (Dalrymple, 2001; Bresnan et al., 2016). Free assignment of grammatical functions enables the existence of discontinuous expressions as in (1).[9] Cases of English extraposition are more constrained as grammatical functions are generally assumed to

---

[9]Again, this does not mean that discontinuity is unconstrained: it appears constrained by information structure. Moreover, there are languages which like Warlpiri have free assignment of grammatical functions, but which lack discontinuous nominal expressions in which two words with the same case-marking are separated. We can say that Warlpiri has *head optionality*, allowing for a modifier to appear without its head nominal.

be assigned configurationally.

In LFG c-structure is licensed and constrained by c-structure rules (phrase structure rules), assumed to be static constraints on c-structure. In English, a rule ensuring that the subject appears pre-verbally and VP-externally is as follows:[10]

(5)
$$\begin{array}{ccc} \text{IP} & \to & \text{NP} \qquad \text{I}' \\ & & (\uparrow \text{SUBJ}) = \downarrow \quad \uparrow = \downarrow \end{array}$$

The annotation on the NP ensures that if the NP is present, it obligatorily hosts the subject.[11] The rule in (5) partly licenses the c-structure in Figure 1. In Warlpiri, with no obligatory annotations for any grammatical function, the c-structure rules are less constrained in this dimension. An example is the IP rule partly licensing the c-structures in Figures 2 and 3, where GF = 'grammatical function':[12]

(6)
$$\begin{array}{l} \text{GF} \equiv \{\text{SUBJ} \mid \text{OBJ}\} \\ \text{IP} \to \{ \quad \text{NP} \quad \mid \quad \text{V} \quad \} \quad \text{I}' \\ \qquad\quad (\uparrow \text{GF}) = \downarrow \quad \uparrow = \downarrow \quad\;\; \uparrow = \downarrow \end{array}$$

The node preceding I′ ranges over NP and V, as either an NP or a V may appear preceding the AUX constituent (which is in I position), as long as it bears a focus function. The annotations on NP and V are different. Relevant for the current discussion is the annotation on the NP: it is unspecified for its grammatical function (in this case, it ranges over SUBJ and OBJ, but this set can be extended depending on the attested data). Assuming that all NPs in Warlpiri's c-structure rules have the same unspecified annotation ($\uparrow$ GF) = $\downarrow$, it is possible for an annotation for the

same GF to appear on two NPs, enabling discontinuity (under the assumption that in Warlpiri syntactic heads are optional). The actual annotation on the NPs is determined lexically, by case-marking.

In English the situation is somewhat different. Discontinuity of the kind shown in (2) and Figure 4 is licensed by the rule in (5) and a rule like the one in (7) for adjunction of CP or PP to IP:

(7)
$$\begin{array}{l} \text{XP} \equiv \{\text{CP} \mid \text{PP}\} \\ \text{IP} \to \quad \text{IP} \qquad\quad \text{XP} \\ \qquad\quad\; \uparrow = \downarrow \quad \downarrow \in (\uparrow \text{GF ADJ}) \end{array}$$

The annotation on the XP, $\downarrow \in (\uparrow$ GF ADJ), maps to the adjunct set of a GF function. Note that this GF is not restricted to SUBJ, as we can have examples like *Mary mentioned **the claim** yesterday **that John is intelligent***. Despite configurational assignment of GFs in English, there is some nonspecificity in annotation here. It appears that Warlpiri adjoined relative clauses (as in (3)) can be licensed by a similar rule with a similar annotation on an extraposed CP (but with the difference that the clause can appear on either side of the main IP). A more in-depth investigation of the data is needed to posit a specific rule like this, but a generalized rule of extraposition seems plausible and would be promising for a uniform approach to this type of discontinuity. Discontinuity involving case-marked nominals and discontinuity involving extraposition have somewhat different underlying mechanisms. We can say that different restrictions on annotations on c-structure rules in the different constructions (and languages) lead to very similar outcomes, namely that two parts of c-structure which are non-adjacent can map to the f-structure or sub-f-structure of the same grammatical function.

6   More complex cases

There are other types of more complex cases of nominal discontinuity involving modification in English, namely extraposition with embedding (in (8a)) (Müller, 2016, p. 443), extraction out of complex NPs (in (8b)) and secondary predication (in 8c)):[13]

(8)   a. **Many proofs of the theorem** appeared
        that I wanted to think about.

---

[10]The subject can also appear in Spec,CP position, for example when it is a *wh*-word.

[11]I note 'if the NP is present', as LFG adheres to the principle of *Economy of Expression*, which states that all phrase structure nodes are optional, unless required by independent principles (Bresnan et al., 2016). An example of an independent principle is satisfaction of subcategorization requirements, e.g. if the subject is expressed elsewhere in the c-structure (e.g. in Spec,CP) then the NP node in (5) is absent.

[12]The reason for assuming an IP in Warlpiri (following Austin and Bresnan (1996), Simpson (2007)) is the set positions of two types of constituents. The first is the verb-like constituent referred to as AUX ('auxiliary') in the Warlpiri literature, like *ka* (glossed 'PRES') in (1), assumed to appear in I position. The second is the constituent immediately preceding the AUX, which Simpson (2007) assumes to always have a focus discourse function (similarly, she assumes that Spec,CP always hosts a topic function).

[13]I thank the anonymous reviewer for suggesting to include these examples in the paper.

b. **Who** did they take **pictures of**?

c. She watched **him naked**.

Extraposition with embedding ((8a)) is a more complex version of example (2). The extraposed clause can be assumed to either modify the head *many proofs* or the modifier *of the theorem*. In the first case, rule (7) applies, with GF = SUBJ. For the latter case we need an extension of rule (7) to ensure that the relative clause can map to the adjunct set of the adjunct of the head, which can be achieved by an additional possible annotation on the XP in (7) of the form $\downarrow \in (\text{ADJ} \in \text{ADJ GF} \uparrow)$.

As for the type of discontinuity involving extraction from complex NPs ((8b)), this is captured by the definition of discontinuity in (4) if we assume that the first part (*who*) maps to the adjunct set of the object, and that *pictures of* maps to the object. The preposition *of* can by itself map to the adjunct set of the object as well, meaning that both *who* and *of* are part of the adjunct set.[14] Therefore this type of example does not contradict the generalizations proposed.

The example of secondary predication in (8c) is not covered by the definition of nominal discontinuity in (4), as there is no intervening material between *him* and *naked*. This construction appears very similar to relative clause extraposition in the sense that a modifier follows the sentence as a whole. Under the current approach this is not assumed to be a case of discontinuity, even if the two adjacent words *him* and *naked* do not form a syntactic constituent. I leave this issue open for discussion.

An approach to discontinuity following the definition in (4) thus covers most cases, but in an implementation of this approach, one might need to consider specific constructions individually to achieve accurate results.

7 Mapping to Semantics

For completeness, I discuss how discontinuous nominal expressions involving modification can be analyzed semantically. The c- to f-structure mapping in LFG via the ϕ function ensures that a minimal

---

[14]However, this mapping does not ensure that *who* and *of* end up as part of the same f-structure in this set; this issue will be addressed in Section 8.

pair of sentences with or without a discontinuous expression have the same f-structure, as shown above. Semantics in LFG is represented on the level of s-structure. Following Dalrymple and Nikolaeva (2011, p. 90), I assume that f-structure is mapped directly to s-structure via the σ function. The direct mapping ensures that sentences with the same f-structure will receive the same semantics. A discontinuous expression and a contiguous expression will therefore have the same semantics, as also pointed out by Dalrymple (2001). This is achieved by glue semantics (Dalrymple et al., 1993; Dalrymple, 1999; Dalrymple, 2001), the linguistic theory of semantic composition commonly used in LFG, which relies on linear logic. Glue semantics associates meaning constructors, instructions on how to combine meanings to form the meaning of the sentences, with lexical items (or in some cases with phrase structural positions). Semantic composition is therefore largely separate from c-structure constituency, which is especially beneficial for the purpose of accounting for discontinuous nominal expressions, as we want the same semantic analysis for two different c-structural configurations. For example, in the Warlpiri example in Figure 2, the two subparts of the discontinuous expression each contribute their own meaning constructors. Before looking at these, consider the f- to s-structure mapping for the SUBJ (the discontinuous expression) of example (1):

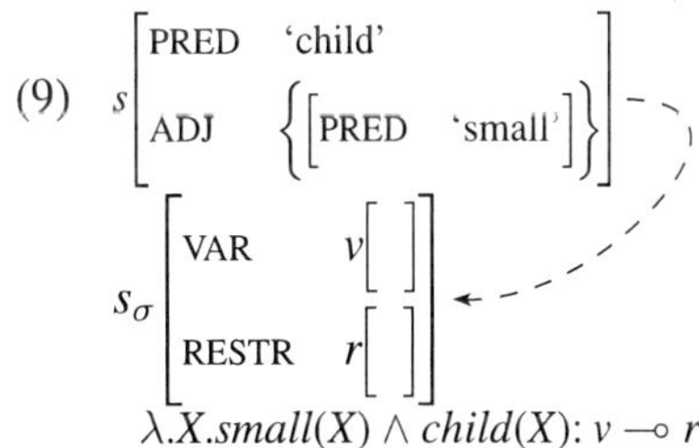

$$(9) \quad s \begin{bmatrix} \text{PRED} & \text{'child'} \\ \text{ADJ} & \{[\text{PRED} \quad \text{'small'}]\} \end{bmatrix}$$
$$s_\sigma \begin{bmatrix} \text{VAR} & v[\ ] \\ \text{RESTR} & r[\ ] \end{bmatrix}$$
$$\lambda X.small(X) \wedge child(X): v \multimap r$$

The f- to s-structure mapping of the head by itself is very similar:

$$(10) \quad \begin{bmatrix} \text{PRED} & \text{'child'} \\ \begin{bmatrix} \text{VAR} & v[\ ] \\ \text{RESTR} & r[\ ] \end{bmatrix} \end{bmatrix}$$
$$\lambda X.child(X): v \multimap r$$

In (9), the subject's f-structure is labelled s, and its s-structure is labelled s_σ. The s-structure s_σ has two

7

kurdu
($\uparrow$ PRED) = 'child'
$\lambda X.child(X) : (\uparrow_\sigma$ VAR$) \multimap (\uparrow_\sigma$ RESTR$)$

wita
($\uparrow$ PRED) = 'small'
$\lambda P.\lambda X.small(X) \wedge P(X)$:
$[((\text{ADJ} \in \uparrow)_\sigma$ VAR$) \multimap (($ ADJ $\in \uparrow)_\sigma$ RESTR$)] \multimap$
$[((\text{ADJ} \in \uparrow)_\sigma$ VAR$) \multimap ((\text{ADJ} \in \uparrow)_\sigma$ RESTR$)]$

Figure 7: Lexical entries for *kurdu* and *wita*.

attributes: VAR which has as its value an s-structure labelled v and RESTR which has as its value an s-structure labelled r. The attribute VAR represents a variable of type e and RESTR is of type t and represents a restriction the variable of type e. For (9) the restriction would state that the variable must range over individuals that are both children and small. For (10) the only restriction is that the variable must range over individuals that are children. The notation $\multimap$, the *linear implication* symbol of linear logic, signifies that if there is an attribute VAR (v) in the s-structure ($\uparrow_\sigma$) then there is also an attribute RESTR (r) in that same s-structure.

The s-structure in (9) of the subject of example (1) comes from the lexical entries of the two words of the discontinuous expression, with the one entry restricting the other. These lexical entries are shown in Figure 7, leaving out case marking. The lexical entry of the head, *kurdu* ('child'), states that *kurdu* provides a value for the PRED attribute in the f-structure, namely *child*. The second part of the lexical entry of *kurdu* makes a statement about the mapping to s-structure (signaled by the use of $\uparrow_\sigma$ mapping to s-structure). It states the restriction on the variable VAR: it must range over individuals that are children. The lexical specification of the modifier *wita* is somewhat more complicated. Here (ADJ $\in \uparrow$) refers to the f-structure of which $\uparrow$ (the adjunct) is a member (the set of adjuncts, or modifiers), (ADJ $\in \uparrow)_\sigma$ refers to the s-structure corresponding to that f-structure and ((ADJ $\in \uparrow)_\sigma$ VAR) refers to the value of the VAR attribute of that s-structure. Likewise, ((ADJ $\in \uparrow)_\sigma$ RESTR) refers to the value of the RESTR attribute of the s-structure (ADJ $\in \uparrow)_\sigma$. Referring to these s-structures with the labels v and r, as shown in the examples in (9) and (10), the meaning constructor premises for the two individual words of the discontinuous expression in example (1) are

[**child**] $\lambda X.child(X)$ $\qquad : v \multimap r$
[**small**] $\lambda P.\lambda X.small(X) \wedge P(X)$ $\quad : [v \multimap r] \multimap [v \multimap r]$

Figure 8: Meaning constructors for *kurdu* and *wita*.

$$\frac{\lambda X.child(X) : v \multimap r \qquad \lambda P.\lambda X.small(X) \wedge P(X) : [v \multimap r] \multimap [v \multimap r]}{\lambda X.small(X) \wedge child(X) : v \multimap r}$$

Figure 9: Deduction of the meaning of the discontinuous expression.

shown in Figure 8, with the meaning constructors in bold and brackets (with the glue semantics side on the right).

From the meaning constructors for the two individual words, one can deduce the meaning of the overall expression as shown in Figure 9. The meaning constructor for the modifier consumes the contribution of the noun ($v \multimap r$), and thereby provides a new meaning, also associated with $v \multimap r$. Without providing a full overview of glue semantics and its use in LFG, this section has shown that by associating meaning constructors directly with lexical items and not with phrase structural positions, one can have the same semantic derivation for both contiguous and discontinuous nominal expressions.

8 Remaining Issues

There are a few remaining issues left to be resolved with regards to this approach to discontinuity. First, one outstanding technical issue that was brought up by Snijders (2012) is the problematic account of discontinuous adjuncts. Discontinuous adjuncts are found for example in Latin, (Bolkestein, 2001, p. 255). In c-structure both parts of a discontinuous adjunct will be marked with the annotation $\downarrow \in (\uparrow$ ADJ), to ensure that both parts map to the adjunct set of the predicate. However, unlike SUBJ or OBJ, ADJ is not a unique grammatical function. This is apparent from the set notation. Any NP annotated with the adjunct annotation will map to the adjunct set, and in principle each NP will form its own f-structure in this set. There is no clear way to distinguish between the case in which two nominals (with the same case, number, gender, assuming that this a constraining factor for discontinuity) form two separate f-structure adjuncts (separate elements of the adjunct set) or are part of the same adjunct f-structure. The only constraining factor in this is 'PRED clash': grammatical functions (including ADJ)

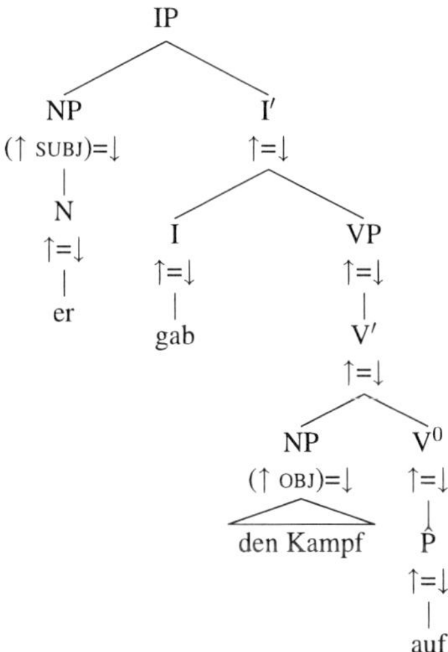

Figure 10: C-structure for example (12a).

may only have one PRED value:

$$(11)\quad \begin{bmatrix} \text{PRED} & \text{`VERB}\langle\text{SUBJ}\rangle\text{'} \\ \text{SUBJ} & \begin{bmatrix} \text{PRED} & \text{`SUBJ'} \end{bmatrix} \\ \text{ADJ} & \left\{ \begin{bmatrix} \text{PRED} & \text{`ADJ1'} \end{bmatrix}, \begin{bmatrix} \text{PRED} & \text{`ADJ2'} \end{bmatrix} \right\} \end{bmatrix}$$

PRED clash ensures that two adjuncts which both contribute a PRED value do not unify in f-structure. Nonetheless, there is no straightforward way to distinguish between the two cases just described, and to ensure that two parts of a discontinuous adjunct map to the same f-structure (or sub-f-structure).

A second issue is that the definition in (4) covers discontinuous nominal expressions, but it does not encompass other types of discontinuity, such as the one created by 'particle verbs' (Ackerman, 1983; Piñón, 1992; Lüdeling, 2001; Booij, 2002; Toivonen, 2003; Forst et al., 2010).[15] Consider an example from German (Forst et al., 2010, p. 229):

(12) *Er **gab** den Kampf **auf**.*
     he gave the.ACC fight up
     'He gave up the fight.'

I follow Toivonen's (2003) analysis of verbal particles as non-projecting words, marked as $\hat{P}$. Example (12) then has the c-structure as shown in Figure

10. In this c-structure the two parts of the phrasal verb both map to the same f-structure, namely the overarching f-structure of the sentence (shown by $\uparrow = \downarrow$). Aiming for a general definition of discontinuity, this makes it seem appropriate to change condition (ii) in the definition of discontinuity in (4) to read '*X* and *Y* map to the same f-structure or its sub-f-structure', with no mention of a grammatical function. However, this rephrasing makes inaccurate predictions, because if we refer to the highest f-structure level (the one of the whole sentence) and its sub-f-structures, we refer to all of the f-structures contained in the sentence.[16] Making reference to all f-structures in the definition of discontinuity makes it impossible to make any point about discontinuity. One solution is to change the phrasing of condition (ii) to '*X* and *Y* map to the same f-structure', but under this condition the English structure in Figure 4 would not be an instance of a discontinuous expression, at least not with the annotations as shown. However, we want the definition to cover both extraposition and discontinuity like example (1), as ultimately both are somewhat different instances of the same mechanism.

9 Conclusion

This paper has illustrated an LFG approach to discontinuous nominal expressions involving modification, i.e. by letting two (or more) c-structural constituents map to the same (sub-)f-structure of a specific grammatical function. In this I follow Simpson (1991), Kuhn (1999; 2001), while making the explicit claim that different types of discontinuity (e.g. two constituents with the same case-marking or the case of extraposed XPs) should be captured by the same overall analysis, despite being licensed in different ways. Crucially, discontinuous expressions and contiguous expressions receive the same mapping to semantics, enabled by glue semantics' association of meaning constructors with lexical items, not phrase structure. This paper has thereby aimed to illustrate LFG's potential in contributing to a potential implementation of discontinuity in NLP systems.

---

[15]Also, discontinuous nominal expressions not involving modification but rather with a separated determiner and a noun, as found for example in Latin (Devine and Stephens, 2006, p. 524), have not been discussed. The semantic mapping for this will be different than the mapping for modification described in Section 7.

[16]One reviewer suggests referring to immediate sub-f-structures only, but the immediate sub-f-structures of the sentence's overarching f-structure include those of the arguments of the predicate, and thereby of the sentence as a whole.

Acknowledgments

I gratefully acknowledge the JSPS for funding this work. I also thank Jelke Bloem, Mary Dalrymple, Ryo Otoguro, Marjolein Poortvliet and the anonymous reviewers for their useful suggestions.

References

Farrell Ackerman. 1983. *Miscreant Morphemes: Phrasal Predicates in Ugric.* Ph.D. thesis, UC Berkeley.

Peter Austin and Joan Bresnan. 1996. Non-configurationality in Australian Aboriginal languages. *Natural Language and Linguistic Theory*, 14(2):215–268.

A. Machteld Bolkestein. 2001. Random Scrambling? Constraints on Discontinuity in Latin Noun Phrases. In C. Moussy, editor, *De lingua Latina novae quaestiones*, pages 245–258. Peeters, Louvain.

Geert Booij. 2002. Separable Complex Verbs in Dutch: A Case of Periphrastic Word Formation. In Nicole Dehé, Ray Jackendoff, Andrew McIntyre, and Silke Urban, editors, *Verb-Particle Explorations*, pages 21–42. Mouton de Gruyter, Berlin.

Joan Bresnan, Ash Asudeh, Ida Toivonen, and Stephen Wechsler. 2016. *Lexical-Functional Syntax.* Wiley Blackwell, Chichester, West Sussex.

Damir Cavar and Melanie Seiss. 2011. Clitic Placement, Syntactic Discontinuity and Information Structure. In Miriam Butt and Tracy Holloway King, editors, *Proceedings of the LFG11 Conference*, pages 131–151. CSLI Publications.

Lionel Clément, Kim Gerdes, and Sylvain Kahane. 2002. An LFG-Type Grammar for German Based on the Typological Model. In M. Butt and T.H. King, editors, *Proceedings of the LFG02 Conference*, pages 116–129. CSLI Publications.

Richard Crouch, Mary Dalrymple, Ronald M. Kaplan, Tracy King, III Maxwell, John T., and Paula Newman. 2011. XLE Documentation. Palo Alto Research Center (PARC), Palo Alto, CA.

Mary Dalrymple and Irina Nikolaeva. 2011. *Objects and Information Structure.* Cambridge Studies in Linguistics. Cambridge University Press, Cambridge.

Mary Dalrymple, John Lamping, and Vijay Saraswat. 1993. LFG semantics via constraints. In *Proceedings of the 6th Meeting of the EACL*, pages 97–105, Utrecht. European Association for Computational Linguistics.

Mary Dalrymple, editor. 1999. *Semantics and Syntax in Lexical Functional Grammar: The Resource Logic Approach.* MIT Press, Cambridge, MA.

Mary Dalrymple. 2001. *Lexical-Functional Grammar*, volume 34 of *Syntax and Semantics*. Academic Press, San Diego; London.

Andrew M. Devine and Laurence D. Stephens. 2000. *Discontinuous syntax: hyperbaton in Greek.* Oxford University Press, Oxford/New York.

Andrew M. Devine and Laurence D. Stephens. 2006. *Latin Word Order.* Oxford University Press, Oxford/New York.

Martin Forst, Tracy Holloway King, and Tibor Laczkó. 2010. Particle Verbs in Computational LFGs: Issues from English, German and Hungarian. In Miriam Butt and Tracy Holloway King, editors, *Proceedings of the LFG10 Conference*, pages 228–248. CSLI Publications.

Kenneth L. Hale, Mary Laughren, and Jane Simpson. 1995. Warlpiri syntax. In Joachim Jacobs, Arnim von Stechow, Wolfgang Sternefeld, and Theo Vennemann, editors, *Syntax. Ein internationales Handbuch zeitgenössischer Forschung: An International Handbook of Contemporary Research*, pages 1430–51. Walter de Gruyter, Berlin New York.

Kenneth L. Hale. 1976. The adjoined relative clause in Australia. In R.M.W. Dixon, editor, *Grammatical categories in Australian languages*, pages 78–105. Australian Institute of Aboriginal Studies, Canberra.

Kenneth L. Hale. 1983. Warlpiri and the Grammar of Non-Configurational Languages. *Natural Language and Linguistic Theory*, 1.1:5–47.

Jan R. De Jong. 1986. Hyperbaton en informatiestruktuur. *Lampas*, pages 323–331.

Ronald M. Kaplan and Joan Bresnan. 1982. Lexical-Functional Grammar: A Formal System for Grammatical Representation. In Joan Bresnan, editor, *The Mental Representation of Grammatical Relations*, pages 173–281. MIT Press, Cambridge, MA.

Ronald M. Kaplan and Annie Zaenen. 1989. Long-Distance Dependencies, Constituent Structure and Functional Uncertainty. In Mark Baltin and Anthony Kroch, editors, *Alternative Conceptions of Phrase Structure*, pages 17–42. University of Chicago Press, Chicago, IL. Reprinted in M. Dalrymple, R.M. Kaplan, J.T. Maxwell III and A. Zaenen, editors, *Formal Issues in Lexical-Functional Grammar*, pages 137-165, CSLI Publications, Stanford University, 1995.

H.W. Kirkwood. 1977. Discontinuous Noun Phrases in Existential Sentences in English and German. *Journal of Linguistics*, 13(1):53–66.

Jonas Kuhn. 1999. The syntax and semantics of split NPs in LFG. In Francis Corblin, Carmen Dobrovie-Sorin, and Jean-Marie Marandin, editors, *Selected papers from the Colloque de Syntaxe et Sémantique à Paris (CSSP 1997)*, pages 145–166. Thesus, The Hague.

Jonas Kuhn. 2001. Resource Sensitivity in the Syntax-Semantics interface and the German Split NP Construction. In T. Kiss and D. Meurers, editors, *Constraint-Based Approaches to Germanic Syntax*. CSLI Publications, Stanford, CA.

Anke Lüdeling. 2001. *On Particle Verbs and Similar Constructions in German*. CSLI Publications, Stanford, CA.

Stefan Müller. 2016. *Grammatical Theory: From transformational grammar to constraint-based approaches*. Textbooks in Language Sciences 1. Language Science Press, Berlin.

Rachel Nordlinger. 1998. *Constructive Case: Evidence from Australian Languages*. CSLI Publications, Stanford, CA. Revised version of 1997 Stanford University dissertation.

Chris Piñón. 1992. The Preverb Problem in German and Hungarian. In *Proceedings of BLS*, pages 395–408.

Eva Schultze-Berndt and Candide Simard. 2012. Constraints on noun phrase discontinuity in an Australian language: The role of prosody and information structure. *Linguistics*, 50:1015–1058.

Irina Sekerina. 1997. *The Syntax and Processing of Split Scrambling Constituents in Russian*. Ph.D. thesis, SUNY Graduate School and University Center.

Irina Sekerina. 1999. The Scrambling Complexity Hypothesis and Processing of Split Scrambling Constituents in Russian. *Journal of Slavic Linguistics*, 7(2):265–304.

Anna Siewierska. 1984. Phrasal Discontinuity in Polish. *Australian Journal of Linguistics*, 4:57–71.

Jane Simpson. 1991. *Warlpiri Morpho-Syntax: a Lexicalist Approach*, volume 23 of *Studies in Natural Language and Linguistic Theory*. Kluwer Academic Publishers, Dordrecht.

Jane Simpson. 2007. Expressing Pragmatic Constraints on Word Order. In Annie Zaenen, Jane Simpson, Tracy Holloway King, Jane Grimshaw, Joan Maling, and Chris Manning, editors, *Architectures, Rules, and Preferences: Variations on Themes by Joan W. Bresnan*, pages 403–427. CSLI Publications, Stanford, CA.

Liselotte Snijders. 2012. Issues Concerning Constraints on Discontinuous NPs in Latin. In Miriam Butt and Tracy Holloway King, editors, *Proceedings of the LFG12 Conference*, pages 565–581. CSLI Publications.

Liselotte Snijders. 2015. *The Nature of Configurationality in LFG*. Ph.D. thesis, University of Oxford.

Olga Spevak. 2010. *Constituent Order in Classical Latin Prose*. Studies in Language Companion Series. John Benjamins Publishing Company, Amsterdam/Philadelphia.

Ida Toivonen. 2003. *Non-Projecting Words: A Case Study of Swedish Particles*. Studies in Natural Language and Linguistic Theory. Kluwer Academic Publishers, Dordrecht.

Non-projectivity and valency

Zdenka Uresova and **Eva Fucikova** and **Jan Hajic**
Faculty of Mathematics and Physics, Charles University in Prague
Institute of Formal and Applied Linguistics
Malostranske nam. 25
11800 Prague 1, Czech Republic
`{uresova,fucikova,hajic}@ufal.mff.cuni.cz`

Abstract

We describe results of investigation of a specific type of discontinuous constructions, namely non-projective constructions concerning verbs and their arguments. This topic is especially important for languages with a relatively free word order, such as Czech, which is the language we have primarily worked with. For comparison, we have included some results for English. The corpora used for both languages are the Prague Czech-English Dependency Treebank and the Prague Dependency Treebank, which are both annotated at a dependency syntax level as well as a deep (semantic) level, including verbs and their valency (arguments). We are using traditionally defined non-projectivity on trees with full linear ordering, but the two levels of annotation are innovatively combined to determine if a particular (deep) verb -argument structure is non-projective. As a result, we have identified several types of discontinuities, which we classify either by the verb class or structurally in terms of the verb, its arguments and their dependents. In addition, we have quantitatively compared selected phenomena found in Czech translated texts (in the PCEDT) to the native Czech as found in the original Prague Dependency Treebank.

1 Introduction

Non-projective constructions in general have long been the subject of research in computational linguistics, especially within the frameworks of various dependency-based theories (Marcus, 1965; Hudson, 1994). In Czech, which is our focus here as a representative of a (relatively) free-word order language which frequently displays this phenomenon, we can cite e.g., (Uhlířová, 1972), (Štícha, 1996), (Oliva, 2001) or (Petkevič, 1998; Petkevič, 2001). However, at that time, they did not have a syntactically annotated corpus at their disposal, let alone a semantically annotated one. Their works are thus rather theoretical treatments with little confrontation with real texts, even though these works have at least laid very good basis for the treatment of projectivity by defining (from various perspectives) what non-projectivity actually is in terms of sentence structure representation.

First treatment of non-projective constructions based on an annotated corpus, namely in the annotation scenario of the Prague Dependency Treebank (PDT), was presented by Hajičová (2004) and this issue was further elaborated by Havelka (2005) where some properties of non-projective edges relevant for the newly presented algorithms were discussed and a hint on finding all non-projective edges using its output was given. Havelka (2007) followed and focused on a refinement of the definitions of non-projectivity (having found certain errors in previously published definitions, among other things) and introduced measures to further refine the notion. In addition, he also showed how empirical results corroborate theoretical results. All of these works have focused on the basic properties of non-projectivity at the same level of linguis-

Proceedings of DiscoNLP 2016, pages 12–21,
San Diego, California, June 17, 2016. ©2016 Association for Computational Linguistics

tic description (i.e., surface dependency syntax *or* the deep, semantically-oriented *"tectogrammatical"* representation as defined in the Prague Dependency Treebank), i.e., the authors limited themselves to only one syntactic layer at a time instead of trying to define and investigate the phenomenon from both perspectives, thus providing a more compact approach. Hajičová et al. (2004) made an attempt at classification of non-projective constructions on these two levels separately.[1] In our work, we are trying to use both the surface and deep layer together to specify and investigate a "new breed" of non-projectivity in a more holistic approach.

In Natural Language Processing, non-projectivity has long been ignored, since the first treebanks, such as the Penn Treebank (Marcus et al., 1993), have been annotated using parse trees (or, phrase-structure-based annotation), which technically do not allow for direct representation of non-projectivity, and the surrogate means (co-indexing and traces, some of which can be considered to represent non-projective constructions) have also been largely ignored by syntactic parsers developed (trained) on them. Only after the development of dependency parsers has started using natively[2] annotated dependency treebanks (which naturally do contain non-projectivities), non-projectivity has been finally seriously looked at from the parsing perspective (McDonald et al., 2005; Nivre and Nilsson, 2005; Nivre, 2006; Kuhlmann and Nivre, 2006; Nivre, 2007; Hall and Nivre, 2008; Nivre, 2009; Bohnet and Nivre, 2012; Björkelund and Nivre, 2015). Since such parsers work with the surface-syntactic dependency trees, there was no specific attention paid to the relation between deep syntax or semantics and non-projectivity.

In our study, we describe the results of investigating non-projectivity of verbs and their arguments, using two levels of description: for defining the constructions of interest, i.e., verbs and their arguments, we use the deep syntactic/semantic annotation level of the available corpus, while for testing non-projectivity using the standard definitions, we use the 'unquestionable' linear ordering from the surface dependency annotation which in turn follows the original word order. We believe this a novel approach not found in previous studies.

2 The corpus and its annotation

2.1 The corpora used: Prague Czech-English Dependency Treebank and the Prague Dependency Treebank

Prague Czech-English Dependency Treebank (PCEDT) is a parallel, linguistically annotated corpus (Hajič et al., 2012). The texts come from the WSJ part of the Penn Treebank (Marcus et al., 1993); the Czech side is their professional translation. The corpus consists of about one million tokens (on each language side) in about 50 thousand aligned sentence pairs. It is currently available from the Linguistic Data Consortium[3] as well as from the LINDAT/CLARIN repository.[4] This corpus follows the multilayer annotation scenario used in the original Prague Dependency Treebank (PDT).

The tectogrammatical annotation of these corpora includes also links to two valency lexicons, the PDT-Vallex (for Czech) and the EngVallex (for English).

The Czech valency lexicon, called PDT-Vallex,[5] is publicly available as a part of the one-million-word Prague Dependency Treebank (PDT) version 2 published by the Linguistic Data Consortium.[6] It has been developed as a resource for valency annotation in the PDT; it is based on the Functional Generative Description valency theory framework - for details, see (Urešová, 2011b; Urešová, 2011a). The EngVallex[7] is a lexicon of English verbs, built on the same grounds as PDT-Vallex. It was created by a (largely manual) adaptation of an already existing resource for English with similar purpose, namely the PropBank Lexicon (Palmer et al., 2005; Kings-

---

[1] The special linear ordering (which does *not* follow the surface word order) of nodes at the tectogrammatical layer of annotation of all PDT-style treebanks will be described in Sect. 2.2.2.

[2] By "natively" annotated dependency treebanks we mean treebanks originally annotated manually using dependency scheme and guidelines, as opposed to phrase-based treebanks converted automatically to dependencies *ex-post*.

[3] https://catalog.ldc.upenn.edu/ LDC2012T08

[4] http://hdl.handle.net/11858/ 00-097C-0000-0015-8DAF-4

[5] http://hdl.handle.net/11858/ 00-097C-0000-0023-4338-F

[6] http://www.ldc.upenn.edu/LDC2006T01

[7] http://hdl.handle.net/11858/ 00-097C-0000-0023-4337-2

bury and Palmer, 2002), to the PDT labeling standards (see also (Cinková, 2006)).

2.2 PCEDT and PDT annotation

The PCEDT is annotated on both the Czech and the English side using PDT-style of annotation. Every sentence is annotated at three, explicitly interlinked layers: morphology, dependency syntax (Hajič, 1998) and tectogrammatics (deep syntax/semantics).

2.2.1 Surface dependency syntax

The surface dependency syntax annotation in both the PCEDT and the PDT (Hajič et al., 2004) assigns a node to each word and punctuation symbol in the sentence. It is rooted in an extra node holding the ID and other bookkeeping information about the sentence. Heads are determined, when in doubt, using the morphosyntactic argument: if a node controls the morphosyntactic behavior of the word directly related to it, for example by agreement, morphosyntactic control constraints etc., it is considered to be the head. All relations (edges in the tree) are labeled by the type of the relation. In the PDT (and PCEDT), there are a relatively few coarse-grained types: `Pred` and `Pnom` for predicate and the nominal part of a predicate in copula constructions, respectively, then `Sb`, `Obj` and `Adv` for verb dependents (Subject, Object, and Adverbials), and `Atr` for all nominal modifiers. Auxiliaries are divided into another set of types, such as `AuxV` (function word-verb), `AuxP` for prepositions (which are heads) and `AuxC` for subordinate conjunctions, to name the most important. There are also 'structural' labels for coordination, apposition and parenthetical relation. An example is in Fig. 1.

Importantly, for the investigation of non-projectivity, all the nodes are numbered by ordinal numbers starting with 0 for the extra root node, 1 for the first word in the sentence in its surface word order, etc., forming a total linear ordering of all the nodes.

2.2.2 Deep syntax and semantics

The tectogrammatical annotation layer is based on the Functional Generative Description theory (Sgall et al., 1986). The structure of a sentence is represented as a rooted tree (as it is at the surface dependency level), with nodes bearing a number of attributes describing their syntactic and semantic properties. Edges are labeled by the (mostly semantic) types of dependency relations, called 'functor's. As opposed to the surface syntactic annotation, function words and punctuation have no nodes of their own; only content words are kept. However, in addition to the content words that have a surface counterpart, there are also nodes which have no surface counterpart (some types of restored ellipses, such as surface-elided semantically obligatory verb arguments etc.).

The set of 'functors' is different (and richer) than the set of dependency relations at the surface dependency level. While verb arguments are described by five core argument functors (Actor (ACT) and Patient (PAT) for the first two, and then the more semantically defined Addressee (ADDR), Effect (EFF) and Origin (ORIG)), there is a set of about 30 adverbial types (LOCation, DIR1ection (from), DIR3ection (to), MANNer, ACMP for accompaniment, TWHEN, TSINce, THL (how long) and several more for time adverbials, CAUSe, BENeficiary, etc.). For nominal modifiers, RSTR and DESC (restrictive and descriptive dependent) are added. Nodes serving as structure descriptors (such as coordination and apposition "heads") are similar to the ones used at the surface dependency layer of annotation.

In addition, every verb (i.e., content verb) in the treebank is disambiguated for its sense based on an inventory of senses in the corresponding valency lexicon (PDT-Vallex for Czech and EngVallex for English, cf. Sect. 2.1). Its arguments as annotated in the treebank correspond to the argument 'slots' as recorded in the valency lexicons. Morphosyntactic constraints on the individual arguments as recorded in the lexicons have been checked and are consistent with the treebank annotation of the corresponding argument nodes.

Ordering of nodes in the tectogrammatical annotation (also a total linear order) does not correspond, however, to the surface word order, and thus any non-projectivity seen in the tectogrammatical annotation can only be judged relatively to the definition of the "deep word order" and thus it has not been used here (for its prevalent use, cf. (Hajičová et al.,

2004)).[8]

3 Definition of non-projectivity

3.1 Dependency syntax and non-projective constructions

The definition of projectivity we are using is as follows (from (Hajičová et al., 2004) and (Havelka, 2005)):

Definition. A subtree S of a rooted dependency tree T is *projective* if for all nodes a, b and c of the subtree S the condition (P) holds:

$$(b{\downarrow}a \ \& \ b < a \ \& \ c{\downarrow}{\downarrow}b \rightarrow c < a) \text{ or}$$
$$(b{\downarrow}a \ \& \ b > a \ \& \ c{\downarrow}{\downarrow}b \rightarrow c > a) \qquad \text{(P)}$$

where b↓a means that b is immediately dependent on a, c↓↓b means that c is a descendant of b (i.e., transitively dependent), and $<$ and $>$ have the usual meaning with respect to the linear ordering of nodes.

3.2 Measure of the degree of non-projectivity

Havelka (2005) introduces the notion of a gap as a set of all nodes that 'cause' an edge to be non-projective, i.e., the head node of such an edge being a root of a non-projective tree. However, in our work, we believe that the mere set of words, or even their count, is too fine-grained to describe the 'degree' of non-projectivity, at least for the purposes of this study on verb-headed constructions. Therefore, we define a *gap* as the number of *continuous spans* (rather than a number of all words) that 'interfere' in (are not part of) the yield of the node, of which the subtree rooted by it is being tested for non-projectivity. We also use the phrase "be in the gap" (for a word or node of a tree), if the projection of that word based on its linear surface word order is one of those that fall into that gap.

4 Finding non-projective constructions and measuring their complexity

In our analysis of non-projective constructions related to verb and its arguments, we have used the definition described in Sect. 3. However, since we are interested in verbs and their arguments,

which are annotated on the deep (tectogrammatical) level, we have modified the definition combining the two layers. The modified definition, named CLP (Combined-Layer Projectivity), follows these three rules for determining the necessary components of the original definition:

- words (nodes for verbs, their arguments and their dependents/descendants) are taken from the tectogrammatical level;

- dependencies (i.e., the structure of the subtrees of interest) are also taken from the tectogrammatical level of annotation (used for determining the ↓ and ↓↓ relations in the definition (P));

- linear ordering is taken from the surface syntactic level of annotation, using the surface node's (referred to by the `lex.rf` link from the tectogrammatical node) `ord` attribute, i.e., the surface word order is used.

While we could have possibly used the surface dependencies for determining non-projectivity, the approach outlined above gives more adequate results since (a) we are focusing on verbs and their arguments, which naturally occur at the deep layer of annotation and (b) this annotation has been done fully manually in all three corpora we use, while the surface syntax has been generated automatically on both sides of the PCEDT and thus is not reliable, especially with regard to non-projectivity.[9]

To illustrate the gap measure as defined earlier, Fig. 1 shows a non-projective construction with one gap - the projection of the tree based on the linear ordering of nodes (i.e., word order in the case of surface dependency syntax) has two parts. In this example, the word "To" (*this*) is an Object of the verb "splnit" (*to fulfill*), and therefore, the subtree rooted in "splnit" is non-projective, since the words "je" (*is*) and "možno" (*possible*) are not descendants of "splnit", and they both constitute the one single gap present in the projection of the "splnit"-rooted subtree.

---

[8]According to the tectogrammatical annotation manual (Mikulová et al., 2006), the linear order of the nodes in the tectogrammatical trees is given by the attribute `dord`, or "deep order" which is defined independently of the surface word order using so-called "contextual boundness" criterion.

[9]In English, the number of non-projective constructions posited by the surface dependency parser is negligible compared to the number of non-projective constructions determined by using the (manually annotated) tectogrammatical dependencies as described in the above three bullets.

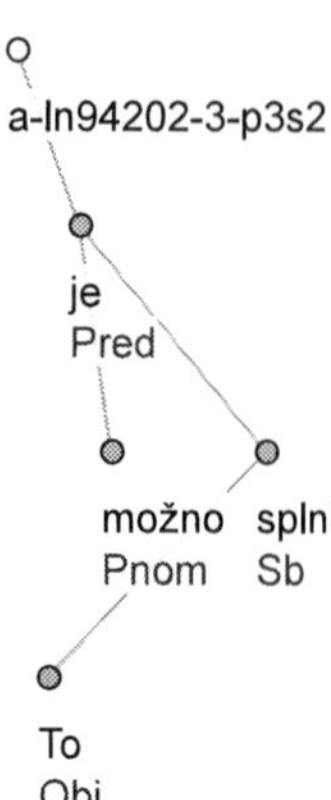

Cs: *To*.Obj *je*.Pred *možno*.Pnom *splnit*.Sb
En: (lit.) *This*.Obj *is*.Pred *possible*.Pnom *to_fulfill*.Sb
En: *This can be fulfilled*

Figure 1: Simple non-projective construction, gap=1

The number of gaps can be easily computed for every node in the surface dependency tree, by going through all the nodes from its yield (i.e., through all nodes which are descendants of the node in question) and counting the gaps. However, one has to be careful–subtrees with no gaps can still be non-projective "inside", i.e., some of their subtrees might still be non-projective with gap count greater than zero.

For the description of non-projectivity of verbs and their arguments, we have thus computed the non-projectivity of the argument-rooted subtrees separately from the non-projectivity of the subtree rooted by the verb in question, which might have no gaps. On the other hand, if any of the argument-rooted subtrees has the gap equal to zero, it is not relevant to our goals whether there is a non-projectivity "hidden" inside, for some of its subtrees. In other words, we consider (verb-rooted) subtrees that have either

- non-zero gap measure at the verb root, or

- non-zero gap measure at any of its arguments.

For simplicity, we will call these constructions (and only these) non-projective, even though we are aware of the fact that we are ignoring gap=0 constructions with embedded non-projectivity.

An important aspect of the extraction was that we have used both layers of the PDT-style anno-

tation using the modified (CLP) definition as described earlier: the identification of whether a word is a verb or not, or whether a word is an argument to a verb, has been performed at the tectogrammatical level (using all content, i.e., non-auxiliary, non-modal verbs, which had a link to the corresponding Czech or English valency lexicon). Arguments to such verbs have been identified using the valency dictionary entry, which lists all arguments by their function label (called "functor" in the tectogrammatical annotation scheme, cf. (Mikulová et al., 2006)). These labels have been matched to all immediately dependent nodes on the verb in the tectogrammatical annotation. However, for reasons already mentioned, we have used the inter-layer links that the annotation scheme contains, and which connect the nodes in the surface syntax dependency tree with the tectogrammatical one(s) to retrieve the original word order and use it as described in the third bullet in (CLP).

This way, every construction of a verb and its argument(s)[10] could be tested against the enhanced (CLP) definition of non-projectivity.

5 Classification of verb-argument non-projective constructions

We have extracted all examples of non-projective constructions for verbs and their arguments from the English and Czech sides of the PCEDT,[11] and for comparison also from the Prague Dependency Treebank (representing natively written Czech texts).

The overall number of non-projective constructions on the surface syntactic level of annotation using the original (P) definition of projectivity and the breakdown by the number of gaps is given in Table 1. The total number of nodes at the dependency syntax layer of the PCEDT is 1,173,766 on the English side and 1,151,150 on the Czech side. The total number of nodes counted in the PDT is 833,193 (only sentences annotated also at the tectogrammatical layer have been used).

The small number of non-projective constructions

---

[10]Unless it is a NULL argument, which has no overt word in the surface sentence as a counterpart; these have been ignored.

[11]For those verbs that are translations of an English verb construction, to avoid constructions which might be too influenced by the fact that they are translations of a syntactically very different one.

Lang.	0 gaps	1 gap	2 gaps	>2 gaps
en	479	112	1	0
cs (tr.)	61,619	44,774	3,827	449
cs (nat.)	29,912	14,259	196	2

Table 1: Non-projective constructions in surface depndency trees, overall counts

on the English side of the PCEDT (i.e., in the WSJ texts) is caused by the fact the the parser has been trained on non-native dependency annotation, and thus almost always prefers projective constructions.

The highest number of gaps on the Czech side of the PCEDT was 8, in five cases (and there was no non-projective subtree with 7 gaps). Overall, there is slightly below 10% of non-projective subtrees and less than 5% with at least one gap.

In the PDT, the overall number of nodes at the dependency syntax layer is 29,912, and as can be seen from the last row of Table 1, the percentages for non-projective nodes and for non-projective nodes with at least one gap are 5.3% and 1.7%, respectively.

When the (CPL) definition is used, the numbers look differently (Tab. 2). The total number of nodes at the tectogrammatical layer of the PCEDT is 757,021 on the English side and 819,206 on the Czech side. The total number of tectogrammatical nodes in the PDT is 593,473.

Lang.	0 gaps	1 gap	2 gaps	>2 gaps
en	11,328	5,561	15	0
cs (tr.)	9,702	4,503	21	0
cs (nat.)	9,186	4,848	53	2

Table 2: Non-projective constructions in PCEDT and PDT, overall counts using the (CLP) definition

This table differs substantially from Tab. 1, giving much more balanced figures due to the manual annotation of the tectogrammatical layer. Based on these observations, we have used only the (CLP) definition for our subsequent investigation.

5.1 Constructions involving a verb and its argument

The overall number of verb tokens tested for non-projectivity in the PCEDT was 92,840. Among those, there are 2,352 cases (1,311 in English, 1,042 in Czech translations) where the non-projectivity involves a verb and its argument (i.e., the verb is in the

gap of the non-projective subtree of its argument) and 1,407 (932 in English, 476 in Czech) cases of two arguments (i.e., one argument is in the gap a non-projective subtree of another argument).

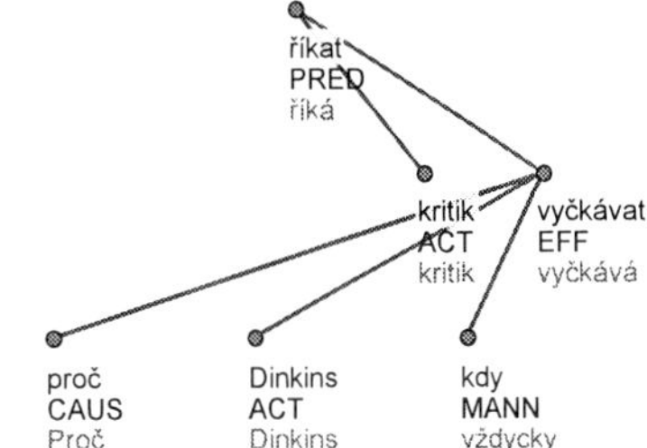

Cs: *Proč*.CAUS *Dinkins*.ACT, *říká*.PRED *kritik*.ACT, *vždycky*.MANN *vyčkává*.EFF ...

En: (lit.) *Why*.CAUS *Dinkins*.ACT, *says*.PRED *the_kicker*.ACT, *always*.MANN *waits*.EFF ...

En: *Why Dinkins always waits ..., says the kicker.*

Figure 2: Non-projective construction, gap=1, verb in gap

An example of a Czech construction with non-projectivity of a subtree rooted in a verb argument, where the verb is in the gap, is shown in Fig. 2 (it uses the (P) definition on a surface dependency tree). Here, the root verb of the subordinate clause "vyčkává" *waits*, which is an argument (labeled Effect) of the matrix verb "říká" *says* on the tectogrammatical layer, dominates a non-projective substree, since the subject has been fronted before the root verb of the whole sentence. This is one of the very typical cases of non-projective constructions, where the main verb is a communication or a reported speech verb (*say, add, shout, remember, answer, argue, go on*, to name a few extracted from the PCEDT).[12]

Another typical example of non-projective constructions in Czech involving a verb is a construction with a catenative[13] (and modals or quasi-modal) verb like "podařit", "začít", "zkusit", "nechat" (lit. *"manage", "start", "try", "let"*), etc. The argument, which is often non-projective, is the Patient (PAT), typically expressed as infinitive, whose first or second argument (Actor (ACT) or Patient

---

[12]Counting on a sample of 100 examples from the English side of the PCEDT, 43 have been of this type.

[13]Catenative verbs are usually defined as those combining with non-finite verbal forms, see e.g. (Palmer, 1974; Quirk et al., 1985; Mindt, 1999; Leech et al., 2012).

(PAT)) is fronted "across" the verb. An example is "domy.PAT nezkoušej.PRED prodávat.PAT bez makléře.ACMP" (lit. "*houses*.PAT *do-not-try*.PRED *sell*.PAT *without an-agent*.ACMP).[14]

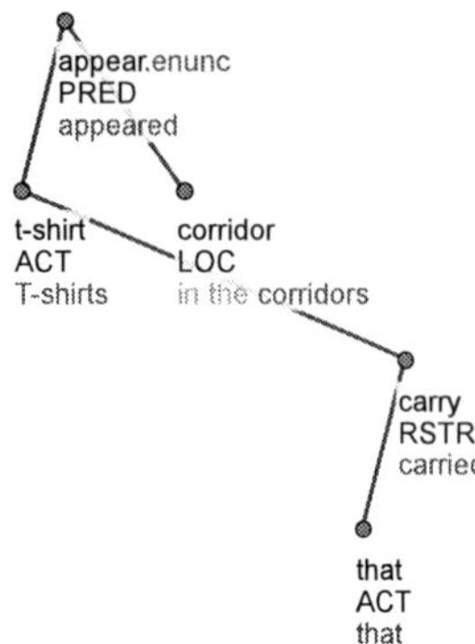

En: *T-shirts*.ACT *appeared*.PRED *in the corridors*.LOC *that*.ACT *carried*.RSTR ...
Cs (lit.): **Trička*.ACT *se objevila*.PRED *na chodbách*.LOC *která*.ACT *nesla*.RSTR ...
Cs: *Na chodbách se objevila trička, která nesla ...*

Figure 3: Non-projective construction with ACT's dependent (RSTR) branching non-projectively to the right, verb in gap

In English, in one of the rare cases where there is no Czech non-projective counterpart, a construction which gives rise to non-projectivity is a verb argument (typically Actor (ACT) expressed as Subject, i.e., in active voice) preceding the verb, which is then complemented by a time or location expression and only then an relative clause dependent on the argument is placed: "T-shirts.ACT appeared.PRED in the corridors.LOC that.ACT carried.RSTR ..." (Fig. 3). Here, in the tectogrammatical representation, "T-shirt" is the Actor (ACT), and argument of "appear", and the clause starting "that carried..." depends on it. In the tree, the subtree rooted in "T-shirt" is non-projective, since the verb "appear" (and all the words from the location adverbial, i.e., "in the corridors") form the gap. Another English example involving a copula is "... opinion.ACT is.PRED mixed.PAT on how much of a boost the market would get.RSTR" where the root "get" of the relative clause depends on "opinion", and therefore "opinion" heads a non-projective subtree with the predicator "is (mixed)" falling in the gap.[15] Another example is "... the plan.PAT is.PRED impossible.PAT to accommodate.PAT", where "plan" is a dependent of "accommodate", which itself is a dependent of "is", creating a non-projective subtree rooted in "accommodate".

In Czech, there are only a few constructions which allow similar non-projectivity to the one just described for English, typically containing the verb "být" as a copula: "... dividendy.ACT jsou.PRED splatné.PAT k 2. lednu.TWHEN z akcií.RSTR ..." (lit. *... dividends*.ACT *are*.PRED *payable*.PAT *Jan*.TWHEN *2 to stock*.RSTR) where "akcií" (lit. *shares* depends on "dividendy" (lit. *dividends*), and thus causes the non-projectivity of the subtree rooted in "dividendy", with the verb "jsou" (lit. *are*) in the gap.

In English, but possible in Czech too[16], is a construction in which a verb argument is modified by two or more modifiers, with one immediately following it in the surface word order but the other being far right, after additional arguments or adjuncts of the dominant verb, such as in: "A total.ACT of 139 companies.RSTR raised.PRED dividends.PAT in October.TWHEN, basically unchanged.RSTR ...", where "unchanged" is a dependent of "total," not the verb,[17] putting the verb (and some of the additional dependents of the verb, such as "dividends" and "October") in the gap of the non-projective subtree rooted in "total".

---

[14]In such constructions, a question might arise how the shared argument between the head verb and the non-finite dependent verb is treated: as has been described earlier, any node elided on the surface (even if present at the tectogrammatical layer) are ignored for non-projectivity considerations due to the non-existence of its word order index, which we in no way try to re-create.

[15]One could argue that the subordinate clause could be considered Adverbial clause depending on the verb, in which case there will be no non-projectivity. However, the distinction between "opinion on [clause] is mixed" and "opinion is mixed on [clause]" has been considered to be in the information structure rather than in syntax (Hajič et al., 2004), and thus the structure in the PDT-style of annotation is the same. This argument holds, due to morphosyntactic considerations such as agreement, more firmly for Czech, but it was applied to English as well by analogy.

[16]Even though all cases that we have found in the PCEDT have been translated using a completely different (and projective) constructiton.

[17]We are leaving aside the discussion whether annotating "unchanged" as a dependent on "total" is adequate for the semantic/tectogrammatical layer of annotation, but at the moment this is how such Measure Phrases have been treated in PDT.

5.2 Constructions involving two or more arguments

These cases are less frequent than the cases involving the verb being in the gap of the non-projective argument-rooted tree, but they do exist.

Similar to the case of verb-argument non-projectivy of the "T-shirts.ACT appeared.PRED in the corridors.LOC that carried.RSTR ..."-type as described in the previous section, is a construction where a Patient (PAT) follows a verb, followed by an adverbial (dependent on the verb), and only then the attribute of the Patient follows: "ABC.ACT signed.PRED an agreement.PAT with DEF.ADDR under which shares will be acquired.RSTR ...". Since "with ..." is an argument (Addressee) of "sign" at the tectogrammatical layer, and thus depends on it, the subtree rooted in the deep object (PAT) argument "agreement" is non-projective. The type of this argument-argument non-projectivity is PAT-ADDR (the ADDR-labeled argument is projected to the gap in the yield of the subtree rooted in "agreement".

5.3 Left vs. right non-projective edges

It is well known that fronting or 'movement to the left' tends to create non-projective constructions. In (Hajičová et al., 2004), it was only such moves that have been investigated, due also to their relation to information structure which was one of the foci in that study.

However, in our study, we also wanted to investigate whether non-projective edges leading to the *right* (both in Czech and English) are rare(r), or whether they differ substantially from those left-branching ones studied previously.

Lang.	left (%)	right (%)
en	1122 (64.93%)	606 (35.07%)
cs (tr.)	913 (68.96%)	411 (31.04%)
cs (nat.)	1,945 (79.85%)	491 (20.15%)

Table 3: Left- vs. right-branching non-projective subtrees rooted in a verb argument

The statistics alone show two things: first, the prevalence of left-branching non-projective edges is much higher in the native Czech treebank (PDT) than on Czech side of the PCEDT (which suggest influence of non-projective constructions on translation), and second, that while left-branching does

prevail 2:1 or more over right-branching, the number of right-branching non-projectivities rooted at verb arguments is substantial (and thus, worth further studies).

6 Conclusions

We have described the results of investigation of non-projective constructions involving verbs and their arguments, using no predefined classification scheme but an annotated material of the Prague Czech-English Dependency Treebank and the original Prague Dependency Treebank. We can summarize our findings in a few main points:

- as a starting point, we have divided the corpus material to those constructions that involve the verb and at least one of its arguments vs. those involving two or more arguments (and not the verb itself), under the hypothesis that these two cases will display different behavior; however, this proved not to be a crucial distinction ("(a tak) transakce.PAT je.PRED přitom.TPAR levnější provádět..." lit. *(and so) transaction.PAT is.PRED at-the-same-time.TPAR cheaper to perform* vs. "(a tak) je.PRED transakce.PAT přitom.TPAR levnější provádět" lit. *(and so) is.PPRED transaction.PAT at-the-same-time.TPAR cheaper to perform*, with "transakce" depending on "provádět");

- the most frequent case is the construction with the communication/reporting verbs (*verba dicendi* and similar verbs) when used in the middle of the direct or report speech construction they introduce;

- nominals used as arguments can have their attribute(s) (whether expressed by a clause or as prepositinal phrase) across other arguments or adjuncts of the verb;

- as expected, certain types of non-projectivity are due to the conventions used in the annotation;

- when comparing native Czech with translated Czech, the statistics on the direction of non-projective branching rooted in a verb argument suggests that translators are probably influenced by the source English and do not use left-branching non-projective constructions as often as they appear in native Czech;

- we have independently confirmed that the focus on fronted or left-moved constructions in (Hajičová et al., 2004) was right, but that roughly 1/3 of non-projective constructions rooted in a verb argument are right-branching and thus not to be ignored in future research;

- certain types of verb-related non-projectivities described in (Hajičová et al., 2004), such as a nominal group in Czech with dislocated RSTR (depending on a verb argument) ("společnou.RSTR máme.PRED ... zodpovědnost.PAT", lit. *"common.RSTR we-have.PRED ... responsibility.PAT*), were not attested in translated Czech (PCEDT), but have been found in the PDT. The same holds for numerals with a dislocated dependent.

In terms of future work, there are two possible directions. In the technological area, the results (especially on English) confirm that non-projectivity is indeed going to be a problem for (deep) parsers, and that even surface dependency parsers should be looked at again to see if improvements are possible based on error analysis using the classification presented. On the theoretical side, we would like to (a) continue to investigate the less frequent cases which we have not included in this study, (b) involve other features of the tectogrammatical annotation, such as the information structure (topic/focus annotation, and/or co-reference information) and (c) define the types of non-projective verb-argument constructions more formally, to allow for an automatic classification, e.g., on a large corpus.

Acknowledgments

This work described herein has been supported by the grant GP13-03351P of the Grant Agency of the Czech Republic and by the LINDAT/CLARIN Research Infrastructure projects, LM2010013 and LM2015071 funded by the MEYS of the Czech Republic. It has also been using language resources developed and distributed by the LINDAT/CLARIN project (`http://lindat.cz`).

We would like to thank to all the three reviewers of the paper, who provided valuable comments; specifically, we are grateful to the anonymous reviewer #2, whose in-depth review helped us to realize and correct several important shortcomings of the original version.

References

Anders Björkelund and Joakim Nivre. 2015. Non-deterministic oracles for unrestricted non-projective transition-based dependency parsing. In *Proceedings of the 14th International Conference on Parsing Technologies*, pages 76–86.

Bernd Bohnet and Joakim Nivre. 2012. A transition-based system for joint part-of-speech tagging and labeled non-projective dependency parsing. In *Proceedings of the 2012 Joint Conference on Empirical Methods in Natural Language Processing and Computational Natural Language Learning*, pages 1455–1465.

Silvie Cinková. 2006. From propbank to engvallex: Adapting the propbank-lexicon to the valency theory of the functional generative description. In *Proceedings of the 5th International Conference on Language Resources and Evaluation (LREC 2006)*, pages 2170–2175, Genova, Italy. ELRA, ELRA.

Jan Hajič, Jarmila Panevová, Eva Buráňová, Zdeňka Urešová, Alevtina Bémová, Jan štěpánek, Petr Pajas, and Jiří Kárník. 2004. Anotace na analytické rovině. Návod pro anotátory. Technical Report TR-2004-23, ÚFAL/CKL MFF UK, Prague.

Jan Hajič, Eva Hajičová, Jarmila Panevová, Petr Sgall, Ondřej Bojar, Silvie Cinková, Eva Fučíková, Marie Mikulová, Petr Pajas, Jan Popelka, Jiří Semecký, Jana Šindlerová, Jan Štěpánek, Josef Toman, Zdeňka Urešová, and Zdeněk Žabokrtský. 2012. Announcing Prague Czech-English Dependency Treebank 2.0. In *Proceedings of the 8th International Conference on Language Resources and Evaluation (LREC 2012)*, pages 3153–3160, Istanbul, Turkey. European Language Resources Association.

Jan Hajič. 1998. Building a syntactically annotated corpus: The prague dependency treebank. In *Issues of Valency and Meaning. Studies in Honour of Jarmila Panevová (ed. Eva Hajičová)*. Karolinum, Charles University Press, Prague, ISBN 80-7184-601-5.

Eva Hajičová, Jiří Havelka, Petr Sgall, Kateřina Veselá, and Daniel Zeman. 2004. Issues of projectivity in the Prague Dependency Treebank. *The Prague Bulletin of Mathematical Linguistics*, (81):5–22.

Johan Hall and Joakim Nivre. 2008. Parsing discontinuous phrase structure with grammatical functions. In *Advances in Natural Language Processing, 6th International Conference, GoTAL 2008, Gothenburg, Swe-*

den, August 25-27, 2008, Proceedings, pages 169–180.

Jiří Havelka. 2005. Projectivity in totally ordered rooted trees: An alternative definition of projectivity and optimal algorithms for detecting non-projective edges and projectivizing totally ordered rooted trees. *The Prague Bulletin of Mathematical Linguistics*, (84):13–30.

Jiří Havelka. 2007. Beyond projectivity: Multilingual evaluation of constraints and measures on non-projective structures. In *Proceedings of the 45th Annual Meeting of the Association for Computational Linguistics*, pages 608–615, Praha, Czechia. ÚFAL MFF UK, Association for Computational Linguistics.

Richard Hudson. 1994. Discontinuous phrases in dependency grammar. (6):89–124.

P. Kingsbury and M. Palmer. 2002. From Treebank to Propbank. In *Proceedings of the 3rd International Conference on Language Resources and Evaluation (LREC-2002)*, pages 1989–1993. Citeseer.

Marco Kuhlmann and Joakim Nivre. 2006. Mildly non-projective dependency structures. In *Proceedings of the 21st International Conference on Computational Linguistics and 44th Annual Meeting of the Association for Computational Linguistics (COLING-ACL) Main Conference Poster Sessions*, pages 507–514.

Geoffrey N. Leech, Marianne Hundt, Christian Mair, and Nicholas Smith. 2012. *Change in Contemporary English*. Cambridge University Press, New York.

Mitchell P. Marcus, Beatrice Santorini, and Mary Ann Marcinkiewicz. 1993. Building a Large Annotated Corpus of English: The Penn Treebank. *COMPUTATIONAL LINGUISTICS*, 19(2):313–330.

Solomon Marcus. 1965. Sur la notion de projectivité. *Mathematical Logic Quarterly*, 11(2):181–192.

Ryan McDonald, Fernando Pereira, Kiril Ribarov, and Jan Hajič. 2005. Non-projective dependency parsing using spanning tree algorithms. In *Proceedings of Human Langauge Technology Conference and Conference on Empirical Methods in Natural Language Processing*, pages 523–530, Vancouver, BC, Canada. Association for Computational Linguistics, Association for Computational Linguistics.

Marie Mikulová, Alevtina Bémová, Jan Hajič, Eva Hajičová, Jiří Havelka, Veronika Kolářová, Lucie Kučová, Markéta Lopatková, Petr Pajas, Jarmila Panevová, Magda Razímová, Petr Sgall, Jan Štěpánek, Zdeňka Urcšová, Kateřina Veselá, and Zdeněk Žabokrtský. 2006. Annotation on the tectogrammatical level in the Prague Dependency Treebank. Annotation manual. Technical Report 30, Prague, Czech Rep.

Dieter Mindt. 1999. Finite vs. Non-Finite Verb Phrases in English. In *Form, Function and Variation in English*, pages 343–352, Frankfurt am Main. Peter Lang GmbH.

Joakim Nivre and Jens Nilsson. 2005. Pseudo-projective dependency parsing. In *Proceedings of the 43rd Annual Meeting of the Association for Computational Linguistics (ACL)*, pages 99–106.

Joakim Nivre. 2006. Constraints on non-projective dependency parsing. In *Proceedings of the 11th Conference of the European Chapter of the Association for Computational Linguistics (EACL)*, pages 73–80.

Joakim Nivre. 2007. Incremental non-projective dependency parsing. In *Proceedings of Human Language Technologies: The Conference of the North American Chapter of the Association for Computational Linguistics (NAACL HLT)*, pages 396–403.

Joakim Nivre. 2009. Non-projective dependency parsing in expected linear time. In *Proceedings of the Joint Conference of the 47th Annual Meeting of the ACL and the 4th International Joint Conference on Natural Language Processing of the AFNLP*, pages 351–359.

Karel Oliva. 2001. Některé aspekty komplexity českého slovního nepořádku. 3:163–172.

Martha Palmer, Dan Gildea, and Paul Kingsbury. 2005. The proposition bank: An annotated corpus of semantic roles. *Computational Linguistics*, 31(1):71–106.

F. Palmer. 1974. *The English Verb*. Longman, London.

Vladimír Petkevič. 1998. Special Cases of Non-Projective Constructions in the Syntax of Czech Sentence. pages 61—66.

Vladimír Petkevič. 2001. Neprojektivní konstrukce v češtině z hlediska automatické morfologické disambiguace českých textů. In *Čeština - univerzália a specifika 3. Sborník konference ve Šlapanicích u Brna, 22.-24.11.2000 (eds. Zdeňka Hladká, Petr Karlík)*, pages 197–205. MU Brno.

Randolph Quirk, Sidney Greenbaum, Geoffrey Leech, and Jan Svartvik. 1985. *A Comprehensive Grammar of the English Language*. Longman, London.

Petr Sgall, Eva Hajičová, and Jarmila Panevová. 1986. *The Meaning of the Sentence in Its Semantic and Pragmatic Aspects*. Dordrecht, Reidel, and Prague, Academia, Prague.

František Štícha. 1996. Křížení vět v češtině. *Naše řeč*, 79(1):26–31.

Ludmila Uhlířová. 1972. On the non-projective constructions in czech. *The Prague Bulletin of Mathematical Linguistics*, (3):171–181.

Zdeňka Urešová. 2011a. *Valence sloves v Pražském závislostním korpusu*. Studies in Computational and Theoretical Linguistics. Ústav formální a aplikované lingvistiky, Praha, Czechia.

Zdeňka Urešová. 2011b. *Valenční slovník Pražského závislostního korpusu (PDT-Vallex)*. Studies in Computational and Theoretical Linguistics. Ústav formální a aplikované lingvistiky, Praha, Czechia.

Machine Translation of Non-Contiguous Multiword Units

Anabela Barreiro[1] and Fernando Batista[1,2]
(1) INESC-ID Lisboa, Portugal
(2) ISCTE-IUL, Instituto Universitário de Lisboa, Portugal
{anabela.barreiro, fernando.batista}@inesc-id.pt

Abstract

Non-adjacent linguistic phenomena such as non-contiguous multiwords and other phrasal units containing insertions, i.e., words that are not part of the unit, are difficult to process and remain a problem for NLP applications. Non-contiguous multiword units are common across languages and constitute some of the most important challenges to high quality machine translation. This paper presents an empirical analysis of non-contiguous multiwords, and highlights our use of the Logos Model and the Semtab function to deploy semantic knowledge to align non-contiguous multiword units with the goal to translate these units with high fidelity. The phrase level manual alignments illustrated in the paper were produced with the CLUE-Aligner, a Cross-Language Unit Elicitation alignment tool.

1 Introduction

Recently, in natural language processing (NLP), there has been an increasing interest in multiword units and in the problems they raise. Multiword units, most commonly known as multiword expressions[1], have been defined by Baldwin and Kim (2010) as "lexical items that: (a) can be decomposed into multiple lexemes; and (b) display lexical, syntactic, semantic, pragmatic and/or statistical idiomaticity". Compositionality is the property that makes the automatic processing of multiword units particularly challenging. Multiword units occur very

frequently with different degrees of compositionality. Some represent free combinations, such as the English noun phrase *round table*, (i.e., *meeting*), some have opaque meanings, where the meaning of the unit cannot be deduced from the meaning of its individual constituents, such as *piece of cake* used figuratively with the meaning of *something easy to do*, or *pay a visit* equivalent to the verb *visit*. Translations of multiword units are often idiomatic and unpredictable and a word-for-word translation may result in poor quality translation (*acid test*). Additionally, in many cases, the idiom does not exist, or exists with a different structural and lexical form, in the target language (*raining cats and dogs*). Finally, the morpho-syntactic properties of multiword units allow, in some cases, the insertion of external elements into the unit (*go for a* [INSERTION] *ride*).

Notwithstanding the efforts undertaken to improve multiword unit processing, lack of formalization still triggers problems with the syntactic and semantic analysis of sentences where multiwords occur and impairs the performance of NLP systems, affecting especially machine translation (MT). Whenever a multiword unit contains insertions, there is a remote dependency that contributes to additional difficulties in analysing and translating that multiword unit. The causes for poor quality translation of lexical and semantico-syntactic phenomena, namely cross-linguistic multiwords and other phrasal units, can be summed up in three points:

1. Current methodologies rely mostly on statistical techniques to train and evaluate MT systems. Statistical machine translation (SMT) models are built on the grounds of alignment

---

[1]This term has also been designated *inter alia* as "multiword lexical itens", "phraseological units" and "fixed expressions", with slight variations in scope and meaning.

Proceedings of DiscoNLP 2016, pages 22–30,
San Diego, California, June 17, 2016. ©2016 Association for Computational Linguistics

pairs acquired mostly automatically. Unsupervised learning approaches adopted by SMT systems use probabilistic alignments where linguistic knowledge is still limited. Inability to identify multiword units correctly often results in translation deficiencies.

2. Shortcomings in current state of the art supervised learning and manual word alignment standard practices, such as lack of publicly available manual multilingual datasets, and lack of linguistically motivated alignment guidelines impose significant constraints on translation quality, because they disregard non-adjacent linguistic phenomena or syntactic discontinuity.

3. Current tools are incapable of assisting, in an efficient way, human annotators in the task of identifying correctly non-contiguous multiwords and produce rules from them.

This paper discusses the aforementioned problems from an empirical point of view and provides a solution for them in an experimental research inspired in the Logos Model to machine translation (Scott, 2003; Barreiro et al., 2011).[2] We use the Europarl corpus (Koehn, 2005) to illustrate the kind of linguistic knowledge that needs to be represented in future alignment tasks, with a special focus on the alignment challenges presented by non-contiguous multiword units. The alignment examples in the paper were annotated with the CLUE-Aligner tool (Barreiro et al., 2016). Even though similar in name to the "clue alignment approach" (Tiedemann, 2003; Tiedemann, 2011), mainly devoted to word-level alignment, our approach is theoretically and methodologically different with a focus on phrase alignment, contemplating multiwords and linguistically-relevant phrasal units. In addition, in our approach, CLUE is an acronym for "Cross-Language Unit Elicitation", where a source and a target language can correspond to the same language as in the case of paraphrases.

2   Addressing the Challenges

The first problem highlighted in section 1, has been addressed by the creation of an empirical basis for identifying support verb constructions in a corpus and understand the impact of these multiword units on translation quality. Barreiro et al. (2014) evaluated support verb constructions by two MT systems, OpenLogos and Google Translate, and concluded that neither of these systems translates them well. Overall, OpenLogos suffers from a weak lexicon, while Google Translate translation errors are more of a structural nature. Although the translations are still problematic, the Logos Model presents an advantage with regards to the SMT approach: the Logos Model relies on deep semantico-syntactic analysis to translate not only contiguous multiword units, such as the support verb construction *to draw a distinction between*, but also non-contiguous multiword units, such as the support verb construction *to bring* [INSERTION] *to a conclusion*.

The second problem reported has been approached by the creation of manually annotated alignments – the Gold CLUE4Translation – which represent an important asset in the development of MT systems. Supervised learning uses manual alignments and aims at taking context, syntax and other grammatical and semantic knowledge into consideration. The Logos Model served as inspiration to deploy this linguistic knowledge into the alignment task through the identification of translation relationships among words, multiwords or phrasal units in bilingual parallel sentences, i.e., sentence pairs that have been identified as translation of each other. It also inspired the establishment of new linguistically-motivated alignment guidelines for pairs of translation units – the CLUE4Translation Alignment Guidelines – that aim to improve the quality of the (machine) translation of multiword units, among other linguistic phenomena.

The third problem was tackled by the creation of a solution for the annotation of non-contiguous multiwords and other phrasal units – the aforementioned CLUE-Aligner[3] – a web alignment tool that places a special emphasis in the annotation of pairs of semantically equivalent non-adjacent structures in mono-

---

[2]The Logos Model underlies both the commercial system and its degraded open source version OpenLogos.

[3]https://esperto.l2f.inesc-id.pt/esperto/aligner/index.pl?

lingual and bilingual parallel sentences. The pairs of non-contiguous multiword units and phrasal expressions can be used in rule development.

3 The Logos Model

The struggles of SMT with multiwords have been reported in several research works (Barreiro et al., 2013; Kordoni and Simova, 2014; Barreiro et al., 2014; Semmar, 2012), among others. Multiword units are a source of mistranslations not only by MT systems, but also by professional translators, in part because they are a source of various contextual nuances, but also because they can be non-contiguous.

For example, verbal expressions such as the English prepositional verb *to deal with* take difference senses (and translations) depending on contexts, typically their object or prepositional phrase complement. If the context of the verb is *to deal with questions*, as in example (1), then the French translation should be *s'occuper de* (*to be busy with*). On the other hand, if the context is *he proved unable to deal with the problem*, then the translation should be the translation of its paraphrase *handle the problem*. However, if the context is *he refused to deal with the problem*, then the translation would be a translation of the paraphrase *analyse and try to solve the problem*. These different nuances are related to the ambiguity and weakness of the verb *deal* and the different meanings of the predicate-like nouns *questions* (*issues, topics, interrogations*, etc.) or *problem* (*difficulty, exercise*, etc.). It is the meaning of these nouns that triggers the different translations of *deal*, just like the verb *take* will have different translations depending on the predicate noun it supports (*walk, responsibility, comfort*, etc.). Therefore, the two slightly different meanings for *problem* in the last two examples explain the distinct paraphrase: *handle* in one case, and *analyze and try to solve* in the other case.

In the Europarl corpus used in our exploratory study not all translations are optimal and often translational equivalents are approximate rather than exact. Therefore, the English prepositional verb *to deal with* in example (1) is translated in the Romance languages as *dedicarse a* (*engage in*) in Spanish, the reflexive *s'attacher a* (*focus on/stick to*) in French, and *centrar-se em* (*concentrate/center (their*

thoughts) on) in Portuguese. The different translations of *deal* are related to the idiomatic ways that predicate nouns select their support verbs in different languages: *take a vow* in English, but '*make a vow*' in the Romance languages (*hacer* in Spanish, *faire* in French, and *fazer* in Portuguese).

(1) *EN* - our Asian partners prefer **to deal with** questions which unite us

    ES - nuestros socios asiáticos prefieren **dedicarse a** las questiones que nos unen

    FR - nos partenaires asiatiques préfèrent **s'attacher à** ([a+a]) ce qui nous unit

    PT - os nossos parceiros asiáticos preferem **centrar-se** unicamente <u>nas</u> ([em+as]) questões comuns

If the different nuances of a verbal expression are difficult to capture even for translators, it is not surprising that these expressions are poorly translated by MT systems, unless these systems integrate semantic or contextual knowledge and apply it to the translation process, as illustrated in example (2). The French MT output of example (1) by the Google Translate (GT) system is a literal translation where no context has been taken into consideration. However, the OpenLogos translation is correct and even of a higher quality than that provided by a professional translator in the Europarl corpus (*s'occuper de* is more precise than *s'attacher a* in that context).

(2) *FR–GT* - nos partenaires asiatiques préfèrent ***traiter avec des** questions qui nous unissent

    FR–OL - nos associés asiatiques préfèrent **s'occuper des** questions qui nous unissent

The precision in the OpenLogos translation is associated with the application of a Semtab contextual pattern-rule, which is a deep structure pattern that matches on/applies to a great variety of surface structures:

(3) deal(VI) with N(questions) = s'occuper de N[4]

This Semtab pattern-rule states that, when followed by the direct object noun *questions* or a noun of the same semantico-syntactic class, the verb is translated as *s'occuper de*, overriding the default

---

[4]Here we only display the comment line of the Semtab rule, not the rule itself or what it does in terms of the Logos language. The rule notation is arcane due to its numeric representation and it would take a larger effort to explain the use and meaning of the distinct codes in the Logos Model.

Pattern	#occurences	#unique
bring [ ] *to a conclusion*	114	84
set [ ] *in motion*	162	140
play [ ] *role*	5165	1216
take [ ] *interest in*	360	163
keep [ ] *informed about*	77	58

Table 1: Statistics from a subset of Europarl.

dictionary translation for this verb. The power of this rule is that it allows the translation system to recognize and analyze multiword units, even when the elements of the multiword units are non-contiguous. The alignment of multiword units to feed a SMT system needs to reflect these semantic nuances, in a similar way to the way the Logos Model uses data-driven pattern-rules to account for these nuances.[5] This proves that alignments that mirror Semtab semantic and contextual pattern-rules of the Logos Model can help create new MT systems and improve existing ones.

4 Alignment of Non-Contiguous Multiwords Inspired by Logos

Non-contiguous multiword units are difficult to recognize and process causing many MT systems to fail in providing the correct translations. For SMT systems, non-contiguous multiword units represent a significant challenge to a correct word and phrase alignment (Shen et al., 2009).

The Europarl corpus contains a significant number of occurrences of non-contiguous multiword units, such as the support verb constructions illustrated in subsections 4.1 − 4.5, which are a source of translation errors due to incorrect alignment. Table 1 shows the number of occurrences for five different cases of non-contiguous multiword units in a subset of the Europarl corpus, containing about 47.4 million words, where the search was performed using all forms of each verb. The third pattern is the most common type of multiword unit and also the

one with the highest spectrum of common usages. About 83% of the forms occur more than once. The fourth pattern occurs more than once 65% of the times, revealing these commonly adopted constructions appear in many different forms. On the other hand, the first, second and fifth patterns occur only once, 62%, 78% and 62% of the times, thus suggesting that learning automatic models to deal with these type of constructions may not be straightforward.

The remainder of this section discusses each case taking into account the Logos Model and showing how each alignment is represented in CLUE-Aligner.

4.1 *bring* [ ] *to a conclusion*

In example (4), the English non-contiguous support verb construction *bring* [INSERTION] *to a conclusion* places the predicate noun *conclusion*, with its adnominal modifiers, ten words apart from the support verb *bring*. The Spanish, French, and Portuguese translation equivalents adopt different stylistic variants and simpler surface structures (i.e., syntax) by transforming the support verb construction into semantically equivalent verbal constructions, the single verb *acelerar* (*speed up, accelerate*) in Spanish or the compound verbs *faire avancer* (*make advance*) and *apressar-se a apresentar* (*hurry to present*) in French and Portuguese, respectively.

(4) *EN* - I would urge the European Commission to **bring** the process of adopting the directive to on additional pensions **to a conclusion**

ES - insto a la comisión europea para que **acelere** la directiva sobre pensiones complementares

FR - j'insiste auprès de la comission européenne pour **faire avancer** la directive sur les pensions complémentaires

PT - exorto a comissão europeia a **apressar-se a apresentar** a directiva relativa as pensões complementares

This non-contiguous support verb construction, with a remote placement of one of the components of the unit, represents a difficult unit to align and to translate. In general, statistical (or statistically-based) MT systems translate fairly well contiguous multiword units taking into account context (surrounding word strings). However, purely statistical phrase-based MT systems translate poorly multiwords that contain elements placed remotely

---

[5]Unlike rule-based MT models, the Logos Model is not rule-driven, but data-driven, i.e., in Logos, patterns, not rules, do the matching. So, in Logos, a rule refers to the action component once a match is made. Like SMT, it is possible to apply the same techniques to the data, which in the Logos Model is not literal words but semantico-syntactic (SAL) patterns or entities. This is the reason why it makes sense to train a machine learning system to learn new SAL patterns based on alignments, instead of on the conventionally used SMT patterns.

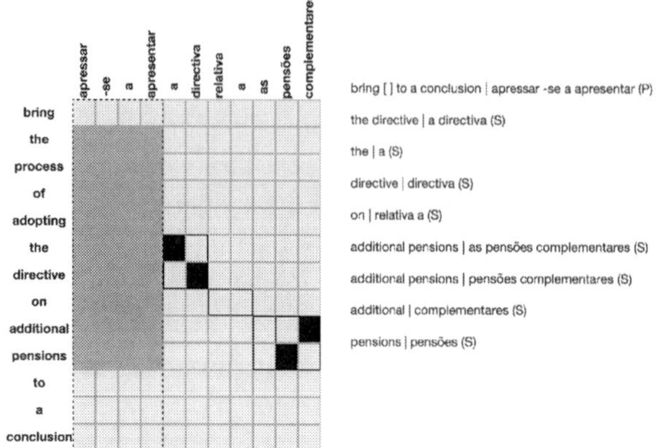

Figure 1: Alignment of *bring [ ] to a conclusion*

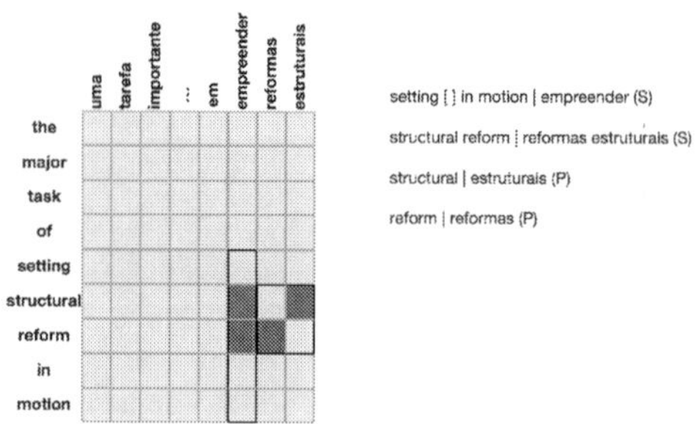

Figure 2: Alignment of *setting [ ] in motion*

(long distance dependency), as illustrated in the Portuguese translation of the support verb construction by Google Translate in example (5), where the verb is missing.

(5) *PT–GT* - Gostaria de exortar a Comissão Europeia a que o processo de adopção da directiva para as pensões adicionais ***para** uma conclusão.

Figure 1 represents the P-alignment of the non-contiguous support verb construction *bring [ ] to a conclusion* with its contiguous equivalent compound verb *apressar-se a apresentar* in Portuguese.

The most common expression found in our subset of the Europarl corpus is *bring this matter to a conclusion* and the remaining expressions occur very few times.

4.2 *setting [ ] in motion*

Often in translation, a non-contiguous expression in a source language can be maintained in the target language or replaced by an equivalent but contiguous expression that conveys the same meaning. It can also be transformed into a simpler contiguous syntactic structure, such as a single word. For example, the Portuguese translation for the non-contiguous English support verb construction *set in motion* in example (6) is the single verb *empreender* (*undertake*). Both Spanish and French maintain the support verb constructions (*llevar a cabo* and *mettre en chantier*), but they are contiguous, having no insertions. The presence of a non-contiguous expression in one of the sentences of the language pair causes additional complexity to the alignment task,

which we are able to solve with the Logos Model approach.

(6) *EN* - many member states thus have the major task of **setting** structural reform **in motion**

ES - he aquí por lo tanto una tarea de gran importancia para que numerosos estados miembros **lleven a cabo** reformas estructurales

FR - il y a donc là une táche considérable pour beaucoup d'états membres, celle de **mettre en chantier** des réformes structurelles

PT - há, portanto, uma tarefa importante para muitos estados-membros em **empreender** reformas estruturais

Figure 2 represents the alignment of the non-contiguous support verb construction *setting [ ] in motion* with the single verb *empreender* in Portuguese.

4.3 *play [ ] role*

In some cases, the verbal expression is always expressed in the form of a support verb construction, which is the case of *play* [INSERTION] *role*, because there is no semantically equivalent single verb. The support verb can take several forms, i.e., the construction can be stylistically different (Barreiro, 2009). Figure 3 exemplifies the adjective modifier insertions *increasingly predominant* in the English sentence. These insertions are excluded from the English–Portuguese alignment pair *play [ ] a role – desempenham um papel* and aligned separately.

4.4 *take [ ] interest in*

Non-contiguous prepositional verbs are aligned together with the preposition. Example (7) illustrates the alignment of the English support verb construction *take [ ] interest in* with its semantically equivalent prepositional verbs in the Romance languages. In this support verb construction, the preposition *in*

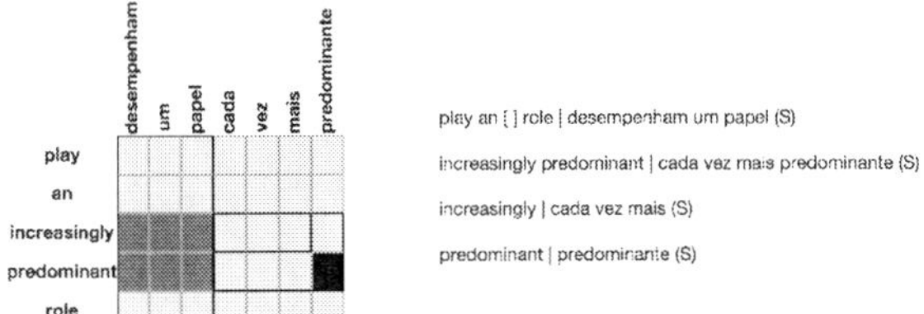

Figure 3: Alignment of *play [ ] role*

is selected by the predicate noun *interest*, and not by the support verb *take*. In the Romance languages, the prepositions are selected by strong verbs: *ocuparse [ ] de* in Spanish, *s'occuper [ ] des* in French, and *debruçar-se [ ] sobre* in Portuguese. The adjectival insertion *special* aligns with the adverbial insertions in the Romance languages: *en especial* in Spanish, *en particulier* in French, and *em especial* in Portuguese.

(7) *EN* - the committee on employment and social affairs **took a** special **interest in** types of supplementary pension funds

    ES - la comisión de empleo y de asuntos sociales **se ha ocupado** en especial **de** las modalidades de la asistencia suplementaria a la tercera edad

    FR - la commission de l'emploi et des affaires sociales **s'est** en particulier **occupée** <u>des</u> ([**de**+les]) différentes formes de retraite complémentaire

    PT - a comissão do emprego e dos assuntos sociais **debruçou-se** em especial **sobre** as possibilidades existentes para regimes complementares de reforma

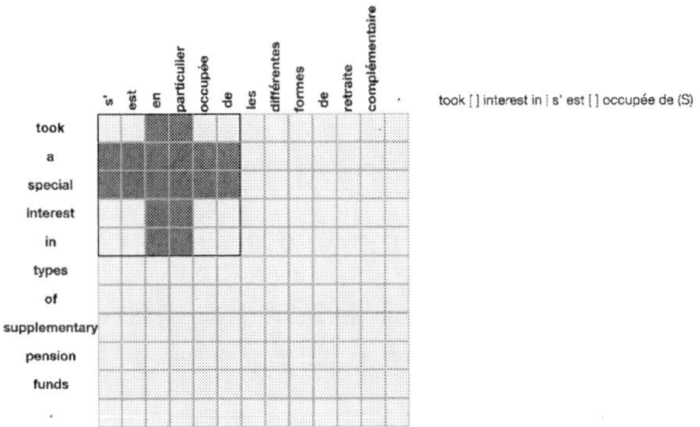

Figure 4: Alignment of *took [ ] interest in*

Figure 4 represents the alignment of the non-contiguous prepositional verb *took [ ] interest in* with the corresponding reflexive prepositional verb *s'occuper de* in French.

4.5 *keep [ ] informed about*

Prepositional adjectives align as internal elements of support verb constructions. Example (8) illustrates the alignment of contiguous prepositional adjectives, with the exception of Spanish. The prepositional adjective in Spanish contains an adverbial insertion (*periódicamente*) between the adjective *informados* and the preposition *de*. In English, French, and Portuguese, the adverbs occur before the prepositional adjectives. Therefore, the contiguous prepositional adjective *informed about* in English aligns with its semantically equivalent prepositional adjectives *informés des* in French, and *informados acerca d(os)* in Portuguese.

(8) *EN* - calling on the commission **to keep us** regularly **informed about** recent developments

    ES - pidiendo a la comisión que **nos mantenga informados** periódicamente **de** lo que vaya ocurriendo

    FR - appelant la commission à **nous tenir** régulièrement **informés des** ([**de**+les]) derniers développements de ce dossier

    PT - em que se apela à comissão para que **nos mantenha** regularmente **informados acerca d**os ([**de**+os]) progressos que se forem realizando

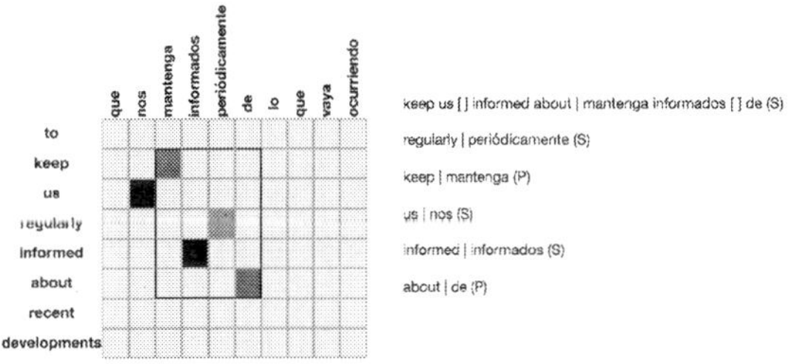

Figure 5: Alignment of *keep [ ] informed about*

Figure 4 represents the alignment of the non-contiguous support verb construction with a prepositional adjective *keep [ ] informed about* with its Spanish equivalent *mantenga informados de*.

5 Advantages of the Logos Model

Former word alignment techniques, even when they contemplated multiword unit alignments, were unable to present a consistent and efficient solution to process non-contiguous expressions. The advantage of the Logos Model with regards to non-contiguous multiword units is its ability to relate constituents that are apart (even very far apart) in the sentence. Semtab is an effective way of analysing and translating words in context, especially when the context is remote. In addition to this, Semtab also allows generalizing between alternative forms of the same multiword, phrase or expression. For example, it presents the possibility of generalizing translations of *take a walk* to translations of *walk*, if one of these two is found in the training corpus. Similarly, closed class items or highly frequent multiwords and phrases might be learnt quickly and be translated correctly by a SMT system, but open class items or less frequent multiwords and phrases might present more challenging problems that can be observed in MT translations, but also in non-native speakerisms, such as the choice of a support verb for a particular support verb construction (e.g., *make a visit* or *pay a visit*?), which can be robustely corrected by the use of Semtab.

Independently of the MT approach, the most important consideration with respect to multiword units is that they should never be processed on a word-for-word basis, because they represent atomic semantico-syntactic and translation units and cannot be broken down into constituent parts in any alignment process. Given that SMT translation quality depends on the quality of the alignments, it is necessary a better representation of multiword units, and greater amounts of training data. Only a more general representation and access to lexica will cause an impact on unseen multiwords. Therefore, linguistic knowledge "elicited" in the alignment process and the use of a more refined alignment tool can solve some of the problems related to multiword unit alignment, when it is so relevant that these alignments mirror the unity of the expression.

6   Analysis of Preliminary Results

Taking into account the search performed in section 4 and the corresponding results summarised in Table 1, we have analysed the first 20 sentences extracted from the subset corpus for each one of the multiword cases. In order to assess the current translation quality of each one of the previously described cases, we translated each sample using Google Translate and performed an empirical evaluation of the achieved results.

For the support verb construction *bring [ ] to a conclusion*, we categorized all 20 translations as incorrect, inadequate or non-optimal. Example (9) illustrates a literal, unnatural Portuguese translation *trazer a uma conclusão* for this support verb construction, where a paraphrase of it, such as *concluir* or *terminar este dossier*, represents a higher quality translation.

(9) $_{EN}$ - The Council is full of good intentions to do all it can **to bring** this dossier **to a conclusion**

$_{PT-GT}$ - O Conselho está cheio de boas intenções para fazer todo o possível para *__trazer__ este dossier **a uma conclusão**

We also categorized all 20 translations of sentences with the support verb construction *set [ ] in motion* as incorrect. Example (10) illustrates a literal, incorrect translation *estabeleceu [ ] em movimento*, instead of *iniciou* or *pôs em marcha*.

(10) $_{EN}$ - it was the Polish Solidarnosc movement which **set** the downfall of the Soviet superpower **in motion** 20 years ago

$_{PT-GT}$ - foi o movimento Solidarnosc polonês que *__estabeleceu__ a queda da superpotência soviética **em movimento** há 20 anos

For the support verb construction *play [ ] role*, we categorized 8 of the 20 translations as incorrect, inadequate or non-optimal. Example (11) illustrates a literal, incorrect translation *jogar o papel*, instead of *desempenhar o papel*.

(11) $_{EN}$ - the European Parliament is not prepared to simply **play the role of** observer

$_{PT-GT}$ - o Parlamento Europeu não está preparado para simplesmente *__jogar o papel de__ observador

For the support verb construction *take [ ] interest in*, we categorized 16 of the 20 translations as incorrect, inadequate or non-optimal. Example (12) illustrates the consequences that an incorrect approach to non-contiguous support verb constructions (and other multiword units) have over translation, which is responsible for the incorrect agreement between noun (*interesse* is masculine) and adjective (*morna* is feminine), but also for the non-optimal translation of the support verb. A higher quality translation would use the non-elementary support verbs *manifeste* or *demonstre*, in the present subjunctive instead of in the infinitive form (unlike the incorrectly chosen support verb form *ter*).

(12) *EN* - It is unacceptable for the Commission only **to take** a lukewarm **interest in** a country

    PT−GT - É inaceitável que a Comissão só a ***ter** um **interesse** morna **em** um país

For the support verb construction *keep informed about*, we categorized 9 of the 20 translations as incorrect, inadequate or non-optimal. Example (13) illustrates an incorrect translation *tem [...] manteve informados sobre* for this support verb construction, which should be translated as (*que nos*) *tem mantido informados*, or (*que nos*) *tem informado*, among others.

(13) *EN* - We have a Commissioner who has played and still is playing a major role in this enlargement, who **has** constantly **kept** us **informed about** what he was doing and with whom we have clearly always been on the same wavelength from a political point of view.

    PT−GT - Temos um Comissário, que desempenhou e continua a desempenhar um papel importante no este alargamento, que ***tem** constantemente nos ***manteve informados sobre** o que ele estava fazendo e com quem temos claramente sido sempre no mesmo comprimento de onda de um ponto de vista político

In addition to the lexical problems related to the translation of non-contiguous multiword units, there are also structural errors, such as lack of agreement (e.g., *para nos manter regular e estreitamente *informado sobre*; *que o Parlamento *ser bem *informados sobre*) and incorrect word order (se conseguirmos ***a** adoptar e defini-**lo** em movimento), among others.

Even though, we have analysed just a few cases, the findings point to a general lack of quality in the translation of non-contiguous support verb constructions, which appear to be also true for other types of non-contiguous multiword units and phrasal expressions. A broader quantification of the phenomenon would help validating our preliminary results. A subsequent work could evaluate the performance of hierarchical phrase-based, syntax-based, and neural network translation models, which have the theoretical capacity to learn non-contiguous expressions.

7 Conclusions and Future Directions

This paper aims to prove that standard MT systems can benefit significantly by assuming a correct processing of non-contiguous multiword units, which current approaches are not exploring efficiently. The amount of post-editing effort can be reduced by increasing the quality of the alignments.

Non-contiguous support verb constructions processing, recognition and translation is a challenging problem when using alignment techniques. Some methodologies are inefficient in the sense that they violate the intrinsic property of the unit as an atomic group of elements when aligning them individually or when not respecting the correct boundaries of the unit.

Another problem concerns manual multilingual alignment scarcity and lack of linguistically rich alignment guidelines. Previously proposed word alignments guidelines cover cross-linguistic phenomena superficially, excluding the important alignment challenges (and challenges to machine translation) presented by non-contiguous support verb constructions and other multiwords and phrasal units.

This paper presented the reasons why non-contiguous correct and non-ambiguous alignment is important, and showed how alignment challenges have been addressed in the Logos Model. This model inspired us to create an alignment methodology that allows the correct alignment of non-contiguous multiwords and other phrasal units, which we were able to represent graphically in CLUE-Aligner, an alignment tool that handles non-adjacent structures in an appropriate way.

A strategic follow-up of this experimental research is to extract translation rules from manually annotated corpora and enhance an initially created Gold standard of manual annotations of bilingual alignment pairs to feed CLUE-Aligner, based on alignment decisions documented in the work in progress set of CLUE Alignment Guidelines. Therefore, future work aims the enhancement of CLUE-Aligner to align and extract automatically large amounts of alignment pairs to be applied to MT case studies, with an ultimate goal to improve translation applications. Linguistically-based alignments extracted from good quality translation corpora can contribute to increased precision and recall in SMT systems, with the subsequent improvement of translation quality. They are also a valuable asset for applications that require monolingual paraphrases.

This paper could not be ended without without

underlining the great importance of paraphrases in the translation process. Future machine translation requires paraphrastic knowledge that allows to choose among possible translations, the best translation for a multiword unit or phrasal expression in the particular sentence where it occurs (i.e., in context), as illustrated in example (14).

(14) $_{EN}$ - It is time **to bring** this issue **to a conclusion**

    $_{EN}$ - We must **bring** this episode **to a conclusion**

    $_{PT}$ - Está na altura de **resolver** esta questão

    $_{PT}$ - Chegou a hora de **concluir** este assunto

    $_{PT}$ - **Ponhamos um ponto final** neste tema

    $_{PT}$ - Temos de **concluir** este episódio.

Acknowledgements

This research work was supported by Fundação para a Ciência e Tecnologia (FCT), under reference UID/CEC/50021/2013, project eSPERTo – EXPL/MHC-LIN/2260/2013, and post-doctoral grant SFRH/BPD/91446/2012. The authors wish to thank Brigitte Orliac and Bud Scott for commenting on the portion of this paper related to the Logos Model.

References

Timothy Baldwin and Su Nam Kim. 2010. Multiword Expressions. In Nitin Indurkhya and Fred J. Damerau, editors, *Handbook of Natural Language Processing, Second Edition*. CRC Press, Taylor and Francis Group, Boca Raton, FL. ISBN 978-1420085921.

Anabela Barreiro, Bernard Scott, Walter Kasper, and Bernd Kiefer. 2011. OpenLogos Rule-Based Machine Translation: Philosophy, Model, Resources and Customization. *Machine Translation*, 25(2):107–126.

Anabela Barreiro, Johanna Monti, Brigitte Orliac, and Fernando Batista. 2013. When Multiwords Go Bad in Machine Translation. In *Proceedings of the Workshop on Multi-word Units in Machine Translation and Translation Technology, Machine Translation Summit XIV*.

Anabela Barreiro, Johanna Monti, Brigitte Orliac, Susanne Preuss, Kutz Arrieta, Wang Ling, Fernando Batista, and Isabel Trancoso. 2014. Linguistic Evaluation of Support Verb Constructions by OpenLogos and Google Translate. In Nicoletta Calzolari, Khalid Choukri, Thierry Declerck, Hrafn Loftsson, Bente Maegaard, Joseph Mariani, Asuncion Moreno, Jan Odijk, and Stelios Piperidis, editors, *Proceedings of the Ninth International Conference on Language Resources and Evaluation (LREC'14)*, pages 35–40. ELRA.

Anabela Barreiro, Francisco Raposo, and Tiago Luís. 2016. CLUE-Aligner: An Alignment Tool to Annotate Pairs of Paraphrastic and Translation Units. In Nicoletta Calzolari et al., editor, *Proceedings of the 10th edition of the Language Resources and Evaluation Conference (LREC 2016)*, pages –. ELRA.

Anabela Barreiro. 2009. *Make it Simple with Paraphrases: Automated Paraphrasing for Authoring Aids and Machine Translation*. Ph.D. thesis, Universidade do Porto, Portugal.

Philipp Koehn. 2005. Europarl: A Parallel Corpus for Statistical Machine Translation. In *Conference Proceedings: the tenth Machine Translation Summit*, pages 79–86, Phuket, Thailand. AAMT.

Valia Kordoni and Iliana Simova. 2014. Multiword expressions in machine translation. In Nicoletta Calzolari (Conference Chair), Khalid Choukri, Thierry Declerck, Hrafn Loftsson, Bente Maegaard, Joseph Mariani, Asuncion Moreno, Jan Odijk, and Stelios Piperidis, editors, *Proceedings of the Ninth International Conference on Language Resources and Evaluation (LREC'14)*, Reykjavik, Iceland, May. ELRA.

Bernard (Bud) Scott. 2003. The Logos Model: An Historical Perspective. *Machine Translation*, 18(1):1–72.

Dhouha Semmar. 2012. Identifying Bilingual Multi-Word Expressions for Statistical Machine Translation. In *Proceedings of the Eight International Conference on Language Resources and Evaluation (LREC12)*, pages 23–25. ELRA.

Libin Shen, Jinxi Xu, Bing Zhang, Spyros Matsoukas, and Ralph Weischedel. 2009. Effective use of linguistic and contextual information for statistical machine translation. In *EMNLP 09: Proceedings of the 2009 Conference on Empirical Methods in Natural Language Processing*, pages 72–80.

Jörg Tiedemann. 2003. Combining clues for word alignment. In *Proceedings of the 10th Conference of the European Chapter of the Association for Computational Linguistics (EACL)*, pages 12–17, Budapest, Hungary.

Jörg Tiedemann. 2011. *Bitext Alignment*. Morgan and Claypool.

Discontinuous VP in Bulgarian

Elisaveta Balabanova
University of Library Studies and Information Technologies
UniBIT
elisavetabal@yahoo.com

Abstract

This paper presents Bulgarian discontinuous constituents.[1] Bulgarian is claimed to be a language of relatively free word order. As a typical manifestation of free word order discontinuous constituents in Bulgarian have not been studied so far. The paper discusses and analyzes the freedom in Bulgarian word order and points out the way discontinuity has been treated within BulTreeBank. We show the results of our linguistic analysis of discontinuous VPs and summarize the extent of word order freedom and word order constraints within VP.

1 Introduction

It is well known that discontinuous constituents are typical manifestation of free word order. It is also claimed that discontinuity is characteristic of languages with rich morphology. Bulgarian shares both of the above features. Scientists, working on word order problems in Bulgarian, debate whether Bulgarian is a configurational or non-configurational language. Most of them share the belief that Bulgarian is a configurational language, but has some non-configurational features (i.e. the free permutation of the elements within VP) (Penchev, 1991).

By exploring the issue of discontinuity in VP we aim to show the extent of word order freedom in Bulgarian and the restrictions on this freedom, coming from semantics.

---

[1] In our definition „constituent" is the same as „phrase". For the parts of the constituent we use the term „elements of the constituent".

The structure of the paper is as follows: In Section 2 discontinuous constituents and the theories of "free" word order in Bulgarian are discussed; In Section 3 discontinuous constituents are presented within BulTreeBank; Section 4 deals with the types of discontinuity in VP and Section 5 concludes the paper.

2 Discontinuous constituents and the theories of "free" word order in Bulgarian

Researchers on Bulgarian word order have so far noticed that there is a greater word order freedom within the verb phrase than within other phrases (Rudin, 1986; Penchev, 1991). Scientists show that the variety of word order models usually is due to the influence of discourse on word ordering. In the tradition of Bulgarian word order investigations, especially in the first half of the 20th century, information packaging was taken as one of the most prominent manifestations of discourse. Thus much of the research in the field of word order was devoted to the connection between word order and information packaging.

Sv. Ivanchev (Ivanchev, 1975) is the first scientist who spread the ideas of the Prague linguistic school in Bulgaria. The relation between word order and information packaging is investigated by a number of researchers (Georgieva, 1974; Brezinski, 1995; Avgustinova, 1997, Tisheva, 2003, Tisheva and Djonova, 2002; Tisheva and Djonova, 2004a; Tisheva and Djonova, 2004b; Tisheva, 2013).

The interrelation between intonation, word order and information packaging is a topic of research of another Bulgarian linguist – Jordan Penchev (Penchev, 1980). J. Penchev aims to describe the main intonation types of Bulgarian sentences and

31

Proceedings of DiscoNLP 2016, pages 31–36,
San Diego, California, June 17, 2016. ©2016 Association for Computational Linguistics

for this reason he uses the information from the relationship between semantics and information packaging. There are several researchers who investigate particular word order constructions, but as a whole we can summarize that all the researchers claim that there is a number of factors from structural (syntactic), discourse and prosodic nature, which affect the word order models in Bulgarian. The different combinations of these factors give rise to a larger number of word order combinations within some Bulgarian phrases (the VP especially), than in others (NP, AP), which is the reason for the researchers to discuss whether Bulgarian is a nonconfigurational language. Scientists deny this hypothesis, showing that the word order freedom in some phrases is an isolated phenomenon, which cannot be taken as a sign of nonconfiugrationality. They claim that within the structure of Bulgarian there is a combination of configurational and nonconfigurational features.

Based on the above mentioned assumptions, all the researchers are on the shared opinion of that Bulgarian has a rather free or relatively free word order, but noone has pointed out precisely the extent of the word order freedom and the restrictions on word order. Also noone so far has studied discontinuity in Bulgarian, so our survey is the first attempt to analyze one of the most frequent types of discontinuous VPs and the factors, causing discontinuity.

3 Representation of discontinuous constituents within BulTreeBank

Investigating discontinuity within a corpus is a good way to investigate the extent of word order freedom and word order constraints. For this sake we use the corpus of syntactic trees in Bulgarian, namely BulTreeBank, which is a corpus of syntactic trees of Bulgarian sentences. Constituency within the treebank is represented via graphs, which are defined on the basis of mother-daughter relation (Simov and Osenova, 2004). Graphs are chosen as close to the context free-tree representation (Simov and Osenova, 2004). In the syntactic trees the original word order is preserved and discontinuous elements are introduced where necessary (Simov and Osenova, 2004). In the examples from the treebank VPC stands for verb-complement phrase, VPS – for a verb-subject phrase, VPA is a head-adjunct phrase and VPF – a head-filler phrase, which has an extracted element, realized outside the phrase.

There are three types of discontinuous constituents in the treebank.

3.1 Functional element DiscA

This is when a higher dependent is realized between the head and lower dependent/s. For the word order to be preserved, the higher element is marked up with the functional element DiscA (Discontinuous adjunct) and is annotated at a higher place with the functional element *nid* (nonimmediate dominance). Then the element DiscA and nid are connected with the same index, seen as a line in the tree below (Simov and Osenova, 2004).

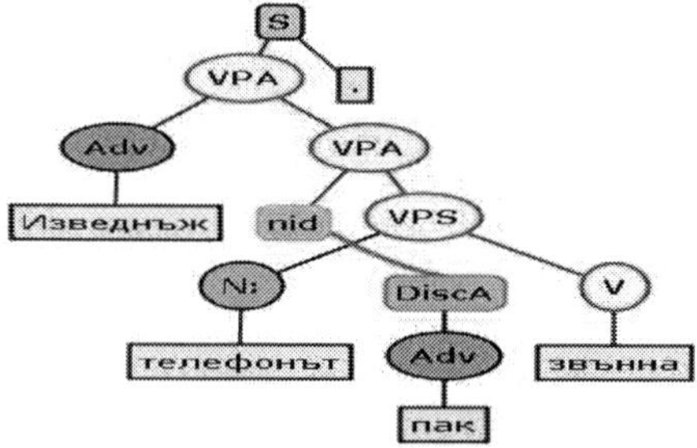

Figure 1: Sentence from the treebank with DiscA element: Izvednazh telefonat pak zvanna. (Suddenly, the telephone again rang

3.2 Functional element DiscM

DiscM stands for discontinuous mixture.

This is a mixture of two constituents. The elements of two constituents are mixed with neither of the two being a governor of the other (Simov and Osenova, 2004). This is a very rare case of discontinuity and has only two or three occurrences in the treebank.

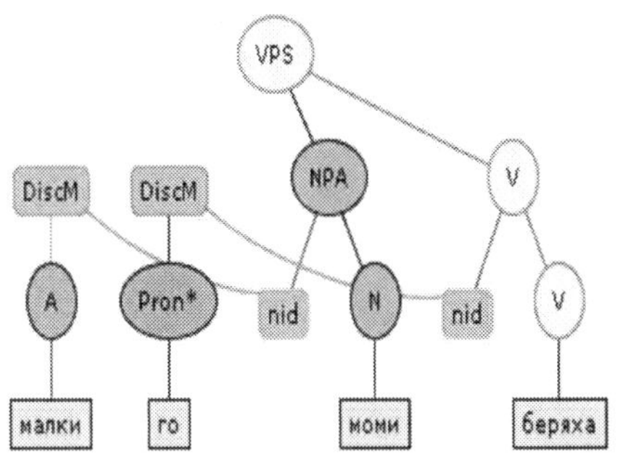

Figure 2: Sentence from the treebank with DiscM element: Malki go momi beriaha. (Little it girls picked up; i.e. little girls picked it up)

3.3 Functional element DiscE

This is external realization of inner constituent. This is the case of extraction (Simov and Osenova, 2004). Again the element DiscE (Discontinuous extraction) is marked with *nid* with the same index as the phrase where it has been extracted from.

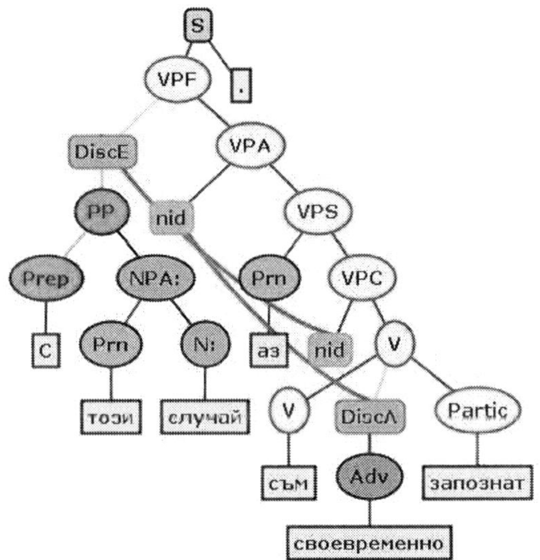

Figure 3: Sentence from the treebank with DiscE and DiscA element: S tozi sluchai az sym svoevremenno zapoznat. (With this case I am on time informed.)

4 Types of discontinuity, based on the type of the element causing it.

In this part we present our investigation on discontinuity within VP. VP is chosen as the most prominent example of free word order in Bulgarian (see Section 2a). For the completion of the task it was necessary first of all to extract all the sentences, containing discontinuous VPs from the corpus. The total number of sentences with discontinuity in the corpus is 4160 sentences, which makes about 35% of all the sentences in the treebank. After doing this, we had to select the types of discontinuities within VP. We found out that there are 2 main groups of discontinuity in Bulgarian VP: i) discontinuity, caused by an element which is part of the syntactic structure of the sentence (the element, causing discontinuity in this case is marked up with DiscA in the treebank) and ii) discontinuity, caused by an element, which is not part of the syntactic structure of the sentence (the element, causing discontinuity in this case is marked up with the tag Pragmatic element in the treebank). In this paper we will not deal with discontinuities of the second type. We are focused only on discontinuities, caused by elements, which are part of the syntactic structure of the tree. These elements are: adjuncts; extracted complements of the head verb and the subject. Here we will focus only on discontinuity, caused by adjuncts.

4.1 Discontinuity, caused by adjuncts

Within BulTreeBank discontinuities, caused by adjuncts, are the greatest number of discontinuities (67% of all the sentences with discontinuity in VP). In the treebank the sentences are annotated along the lines of HPSG (Pollard and Sag 1994). Thus, according to the theoretical frame we use, adjuncts are attached as sisters of the saturated VP phrase, i.e. when the verb has realized its dependents – complement/s and subject (if there is a subject in the sentence, since Bulgarian is a pro-drop language). Only after the verb has taken its dependents and formed either a VPC (verb-complement phrase) or a VPS (verb-subject phrase), the adjunct is attached to this VPC or VPS phrase, forming a VPA phrase. This is the usual case, when adjuncts are realized linearly without causing discontinuity. In this linear realization of the adjunct the latter modifies semantically the saturated VP. On the contrary, in the cases of discontinuities the adjuncts are realized linearly first and the dependents of the verb (subject and/or complements) – afterwards. In such sentences the projection of the VPA phrase is higher up in the tree and the linear intersection is seen as a line in the graph (see Section 3.1). There are two cases of discontinuity in VP, caused by adjunct: i) The adjunct is realized between the subject and the head verb; ii) The adjunct is realized between the head verb and the complement.

Before starting the linguistic analysis, we came across one problem. Namely, the adjuncts were not classified by types in the treebank. Therefore, we needed to have a classification of adjuncts first and then annotate manually all the adjuncts in the sentences of discontinuities, according to this classification. Only afterwards we could extract the sentences with discontinuities by types of the adjuncts. The classification of adjuncts we used is based on GSBKE (GSBKE, 1983) and contains the following types of adjuncts: adjuncts of time, of manner, of quantity and degree, of place, adjuncts of second predication, of condition, of reason, and of aim. In all the sentences with adjunct, causing discontinuity, we annotated the adjuncts manually along this classification. Then it was possible to extract the groups of discontinuities by the type of the adjunct. This allowed us to make conclusions about the reasons, causing discontinuous linear realization of the elements of the VP.

4.1.1 Discontinuity between the subject and the head verb

This is the biggest group of sentences with discontinuities, caused by adjuncts.

Here is the proportional distribution of sentences with adjuncts, causing discontinuity between the subject and the head verb in VP: Adjuncts of time – 45%; Adjunts of manner – 31%; Adjuncts of quantity and degree – 11%; Adjuncts of place – 5%; Adjuncts of second predication – 3%; Adjuncts of condition – 2%; Adjuncts of reason – 1%; Adjuncts of aim – less than 1%

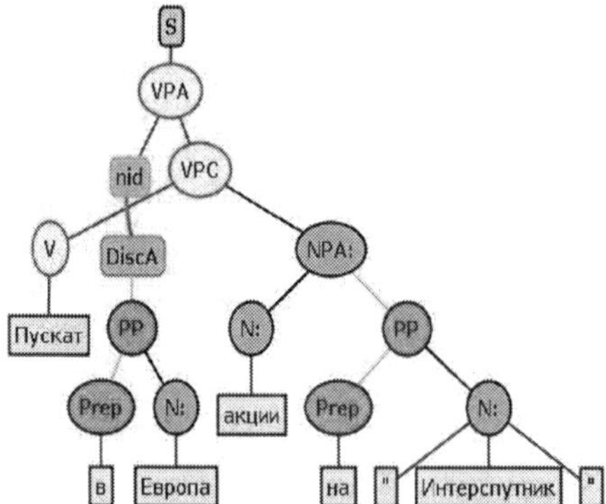

Figure 4: Sentence from the treebank with adjunct between the head verb and the complement: Puskat v Evropa (adjunct of place) akcii na Intersputnik.(They release in Europe shares of Intersputnik).

The information packaging[2] in this type of sentences follows two main patterns:

1) The adjunct is part of the Ground.

Example: Ground [link[V tzivilizovania sviat] tail [chovek **prez celia si zhivot** (adjunct of time)]] Focus [pazi „svetaia svetih" na svoiata reputacia – svoeto kreditno dosie]. (In the civilized world one, during his whole life, keeps the most precious of his reputation – his credit history.)

In sentences with such discontinuity and communicatively marked word order[3] the adjunct can take the information value of either *tail*, or *link of the tail*. In sentences with communicatively unmarked word order the information value of the adjunct is only a *tail*.

2) The adjunct is part of the Focus

---

[2] For analysis of information packaging we use the methodology of Engdahl and Vallduvi (Engdahl and Vallduvi, 1994; Engdahl and Vallduvi 1996), where **Focus** is the actual information of the sentence, **Ground** is what is presupposed by the information at the output. Sentences have **Ground** only if the context ensures it. The **Link** is the particular place in the sentence for introduction of the new information and the **Tail** points out that there is a need for information update in this part of the discourse.

[3] For the relation between word order and information packaging we use the model of T. Avgustinova (Avgustinova, 1997), in which there are 4 types of word order, according to the information packaging: communicatively unmarked, parenthetical, communicatively marked and emphatic.

Example: Ground [Vseki opit za ocenka na organiziranata prestapnost v izmereniata na nacionalnata sigurnost] Focus [**zadalzhitelno (adjunct of manner)** predpolaga predvaritelno da se utochniat obhvatyt i sadarzhanieto na samoto poniatie. (Any attempt to estimate the organized crime in the context of the national security obligatorily presupposes to define content of the notion itself.)

4.1.2 Discontinuity between the head verb and the complement

The position right after the head verb in VP has been investigated by a number of researchers (Rudin, 1986, Avgustinova, 1997, Penchev in: Boyadzhiev, Kutzarov, Penchev, 1999, Tisheva, 2000, Tisheva, 2013).

Here is the proportional distribution of sentences with adjuncts, causing discontinuity between the subject and the head verb in VP: Adjuncts of manner – 40%; Adjunts of time – 30%; Adjuncts of quantity and degree – 11%; Adjuncts of place – 9%; Adjuncts of second predication – 4%; Adjuncts of aim – 2%; juncts of condition – less than 1%; Adjuncts of reason – less than 1%.

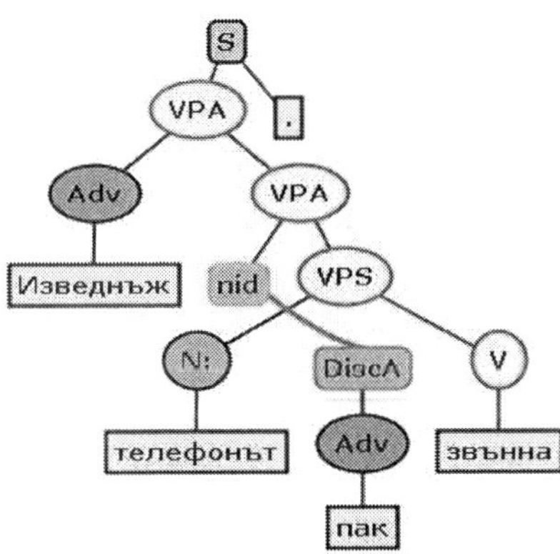

Figure 5: Sentence from the treebank with adjunct between the subject and the head verb: Izvendazh telefonat pak (adjunct of manner) zvynna.(Suddenly the telephone again rang).

In sentences with adjuncts between the head verb and the complement the adjunct becomes part of the focus.

Example: Razbira se, choveshko e da se sbyrka, no tuk Focus [znam **mnogo dobre** (adjunct of manner) za kakvo stava duma]. (Of course, it's human to make mistakes, but I know exactly of what we're talking about.)

4.2 Conclusion about the word order models with discontinuity, caused by adjuncts

From our linguistic analysis we can summarize that the factors, which rule the realization of adjuncts within VP are:

1. The information packaging within the sentence, which depends on

2. The semantics of the adjuncts. According to the semantics of the adjunct and according to which part of the sentence the adjunct is syntactically attached, we distinguish4 two types of adjuncts: i) sentential (they modify semantically the whole sentence) and ii) phrasal (they modify semantically a particular element of the VP).

Most of the adjuncts in Bulgarian modify semantically the whole sentence (these are the adjuncts of time, of place, of condition, of reason and of aim). Syntactically, these adjuncts are realized as sisters of the saturated VP. Thus their linear realization within VP is only a result of the particular information packaging that the speaker chooses to make in his utterance.

The word order realization of the phrasal adjuncts (adjuncts of manner, of quantity and degree and adjuncts of second predication) is restricted by semantic constraints. The semantic scope of these adjuncts – i.e. over a particular element of the VP[5] – demands that they are realized in contact to the element they semantically modify (the contact position can be pre- or postposition).

Since discontinuous constituents are a typical manifestation of free word order, we can summarize that the word order freedom within Bulgarian VP is a result of different information packaging. The constraints on word order, though, come from semantics. This means that whenever adjuncts with narrow sematic scope are realized within VP, their semantics poses restrictions on word order since the adjunct has to be realized in contact to the element of the VP it semantically modifies. The realization of the adjunct in contact to the element it modifies semantically (in pre- or postposition to

---

[4] This distinction is already known for other languages, but the author is the first one who defines it for Bulgarian.

[5] For this we use the term "narrow semantic scope".

this element) results in syntactic discontinuity of the phrase.

5 Conclusion

In this paper we have reviewed the theories about Bulgarian word order in the limelight of discontinuous constituents. We have shown how discontinuous constituents have been presented within BulTreeBank. We have also pointed out the types of discontinuous constituents and presented our linguistic analysis of the discontinuities, caused by adjuncts. We have described the reasons for linear realization of adjuncts within VP and we have also summarized the factors, which trigger word order freedom and impose word order constraints on the elements of VP, thus pointing out the precise extent of word order freedom in Bulgarian, which had not been studied thoroughly so far.

References

Tanya Avgustinova. 1997. *Word order and clitics in Bulgarian*. Saarbrucken dissertations in computational linguistics and language technology. Vol. 5. Universität des Saarlandes.

Stefan Brezinski. 1995. *Kratak balgarski sintaksis*. UI „Sv.Kliment Ohridski". Sofia

BulTreeBank. http://www.BulTreeBank.org/

Engdahl and Vallduvi 1994. *Information packaging and grammar architecture: A constraint-based approach*. In E. Engdahl, editor, Integration Information Structure into Constraint-based and Categorial Approaches, volume R.1.3.B of DYANA, Edinburgh, 41-79.

Engdahl and Vallduvi 1996. *Information packaging in HPSG*. In Grover and Vallduvi, 1996, 113-128.

Elena Georgieva. 1974. *Slovored na prostoto izrechenie v balgarskia knizhoven ezik*. Izd.BAN.Sofia

GSBKE, 1983. *Gramatika na savremennia balgarski knizhoven ezik*. 1983 Tom 3. Izd.BAN. Sofia.

Svetomir Ivanchev. 1957. *Nabljudenia varhu upotrebata na chlena*. In: Sv.Ivanchev. Prinosi v balgarskoto i slavianskoto ezikoznanie. Sofia. 1978

Jordan Penchev. 1980. *Osnovni intonacionni konturi v balgarskoto izrechenie*. Izd. BAN. Sofia

Jordan Penchev. 1991. Nekonfiguracionni iavlenia v balgarskia sintaksis, sp. Balgarski ezik, kn.6, Izd. BAN. Sofia. Bulgaria

Carl Pollard and Ivan Sag. 1994. *Head-Driven Phrase Structure Grammar*. The University of Chicago Press.

Katrin Rudin. 1986. *Aspects of Bulgarian syntax: complementizers and wh-constructions*. Slavica Publishers, Inc.

Kiril Simov and Petya Osenova. 2004. *BTB-TR05: BulTreeBank Stylebook*. http://www.BulTreeBank.org/TechRep/BTB-TR05.pdf

Jovka Tisheva. 2003. *Bulgarian yes-no questions with particles nali and nima*. In: Investigations into Formal Slavic Linguistics. Contributions of the 4th European Conference in Formal Description of Slavic Languages. Peter Kosta, Janna Blaszczak, Jens Frasek, Ljudmila Geist, Marzena Zygis (eds.). Peter Lang, Europaischer Verlag der Wissenschaften, Frankfurt am Main, 715-729

Jovka Tisheva. 2013. *Pragmatichni aspekti na ustnata rech*. Litera et Lingua Series Dissertations. http://slav.uni-sofia.bg/naum/liliseries/diss/2013/3

Jovka Tisheva, Marina Djonova. 2002. *Information structure and clitics in TreeBanks*. In: Proceedings of the First Workshop on Treebanks and Linguistic Theories (TLT 2002). Sozopol. Bulgaria.

Jovka Tisheva, Marina Djonova. 2004a. *Stariat nov topic*. In: VII Nacionalni slavistichni chetenia. Sofia.

Jovka Tisheva, Marina Djonova. 2004b. *Za niakoi slovoredni modeli za topicalizacia na razgovornata rech*. In: Sedma nauchna konferencia po problemite na razgovornata rech. Veliko Tarnovo.

Discontinuous Genitives in Hindi/Urdu

Sebastian Sulger
Department of Linguistics
University of Konstanz
`sebastian.sulger@uni-konstanz.de`

Abstract

This paper discusses genitive phrases in Hindi/Urdu in general and puts a particular focus on genitive scrambling, a process whereby the basic order of constituents is changed. In Hindi/Urdu, genitive phrases may not only occur at different structural positions within the NP that they modify; under the right circumstances, they can also be found outside of the NP, yielding discontinuous structures. The theoretical challenge is to identify and formalize the linguistic constraints that govern genitive scrambling. Further, a successful computational treatment correctly attaches the genitive phrase to its head NP. I use a Lexical-Functional Grammar to solve both challenges, demonstrating that the constraints can be aptly formulated using a functional uncertainty path. Successful attachment further depends on the morphological agreement of the genitive phrase with its head. On a theoretical level, the present contribution sheds light on the possibilities of NP discontinuities in a morphologically rich language like Hindi/Urdu.

1 Introduction

Discontinuous constituents offer particular challenges for various NLP applications, such as question-answering, coreference resolution or topic modeling. This paper relates to an application that is further up the NLP toolchain: syntactic parsing. Here, the main challenges lie in:

- adapting the parser to be able to process the discontinuous structures;

- reconstruct the dependencies in the analysis, i.e., attach the discontinuous parts to their syntactic heads.

Third, from a theoretical linguistic point of view, one would also want to derive generalizations about what kinds of discontinuities are possible, and what kinds do not appear. Depending on the language studied, investigating such constraints is helpful since they can provide cross-linguistic insight into the phenomenon of discontinuity, and why it can or cannot take place.

This paper presents a study of discontinuous NPs in the morphologically-rich South Asian language Hindi/Urdu.[1] The focus is on genitive NP modifiers, which display a large deal of discontinuity. As will be seen below, in the right configurations, they may be scrambled out of their NP domain, removing them from the heads that they modify. Neither the phenomenon itself nor the configurations that allow for it have been previously discussed in the literature.

The paper contributes to solving all three of the above challenges. It discusses the empirical properties of the Hindi/Urdu genitive in general as well as genitive discontinuity, investigated by collecting data from native speakers and searching the

---

[1]The two languages Hindi and Urdu are so closely related that many researchers in linguistics treat them as a single language, Hindi/Urdu. Differences between Urdu and Hindi are mainly in the script (Urdu uses a version of Arabic script, while Hindi uses *Devanagari*) as well as in the vocabulary (Urdu uses more Persian and Arabic vocabulary, and Hindi evolved from Sanskrit). There are further minor differences in the phonology as well as in the derivational morphology; the syntax is almost identical.

Proceedings of DiscoNLP 2016, pages 37–46,
San Diego, California, June 17, 2016. ©2016 Association for Computational Linguistics

Hindi/Urdu Treebank (Bhatt et al., 2009) (§2,3,4). I arrive at a couple of theoretical generalizations, which can be aptly formulated via functional uncertainty within the framework of Lexical-Functional Grammar (LFG, Dalrymple (2001)). I suggest that the possibility of the genitive to appear outside its NP is a result of the rich agreement between the genitive case marker and the NP head. Finally, I describe how the Hindi/Urdu ParGram grammar (Butt and King, 2007; Bögel et al., 2009), a computational LFG grammar developed as part of the ParGram project (Sulger et al., 2013; Butt et al., 2002) and implemented in XLE (Crouch et al., 2015), is adapted to parse and correctly attach discontinuous genitives to their NPs (§5).[2] The paper concludes in §6.

2 General Description

The genitive case in Hindi/Urdu is realized using the clitic *k-*, which is attached to a possessor NP. Under the analysis of Hindi/Urdu case in Butt and King (2004), which I adapt here, all case clitics functionally head a KP (*case phrase*).[3] The genitive differs from other case clitics: it agrees in number, gender and morphological form (nominative or oblique) with the head noun, the possessum. For the feminine, there is morphological syncretism in that a single form *ki* is used throughout the feminine inflectional pattern. For the masculine, there is syncretism between the singular oblique and plural nominative and oblique. Table 1 shows the complete pattern of the clitic. In (1)–(3), the a. examples are valid NPs, displaying the correct agreement pattern.

(1)   a.   ram=ka   makan
          Ram.M.SG=GEN.M.SG house.M.SG
          'Ram's house'

      b.   * ram=ki
          Ram.M.SG=GEN.F.SG/PL
          makan
          house.M.SG

      c.   * ram=ke   makan
          Ram.M.SG=GEN.M.PL house.M.SG

Gender	Number	Inflection	Form
Masculine	Singular	Nominative	*ka*
		Oblique	*ke*
	Plural	Nominative	*ke*
		Oblique	*ke*
Feminine	Singular	Nominative	*ki*
		Oblique	*ki*
	Plural	Nominative	*ki*
		Oblique	*ki*

Table 1: Possible inflections of Hindi/Urdu genitive case clitic *k-*

(2)   a.   nina=ki   beti
          Nina.F.SG=GEN.F.SG daughter.F.SG
          'Ram's car'

      b.   * nina=ka   beti
          Nina.F.SG=GEN.M.SG daughter.F.SG

      c.   * nina=ke   beti
          Nina.F.SG=GEN.M.PL daughter.F.SG

(3)   a.   nadya=ke   bete
          Nadya.F.SG=GEN.M.PL son.M.PL
          'Nadya's sons'

      b.   * nadya=ka   bete
          Nadya.F.SG=GEN.M.SG son.M.PL

      c.   * nadya=ki   bete
          Nadya.F.SG=GEN.F.SG/PL son.M.PL

Within NPs, the modifying possessor phrase comes first, then the possessum (i.e., the head of the NP); this conforms to the general clausal word order in Hindi/Urdu, which is head-final (Mohanan, 1994; Butt, 1995). The position of the genitive phrase varies with respect to other NP modifiers, such as adjectives or quantifiers; see (4) for an example. NP modifiers occurring after the NP head are judged as ungrammatical by the informants; see (4c) for an example. Another example illustrating the variable word order inside the NP is shown in (5).

(4)   a.   ram=ki   nili
          Ram.M.SG=GEN.F.SG blue.F.SG
          gari
          car.F.SG
          'Ram's blue car'

      b.   nili   ram=ki
          blue.F.SG Ram.M.SG=GEN.F.SG

---

[2]The Hindi/Urdu ParGram grammar can be tested using the INESS website at `http://iness.uib.no/`.

[3]The status of the case marker as a clitic is not of direct importance here; the interested reader is referred to Butt and King (2004) for a comprehensive discussion.

gari
car.F.SG

'Ram's blue car'

c. * nili   gari
blue.F.SG car.F.SG
ram=ki
Ram.M.SG=GEN.F.SG

(5) a. ustad=ka   kʊch hoʃyar
teacher.M.SG=GEN.M.SG some smart
talɪb-ɪlm
student.M.PL

'some smart students of the teacher'

b. ustad=ka hoʃyar kʊch talɪb-ɪlm

c. kʊch ustad=ka hoʃyar talɪb-ɪlm

d. kʊch hoʃyar ustad=ka talɪb-ɪlm

e. hoʃyar kʊch ustad=ka talɪb-ɪlm

f. hoʃyar ustad=ka kʊch talɪb-ɪlm

The constraint that NP modifiers have to precede their head inside the NP is corroborated by data such as in (6b) (a permutation of (6a)). Here, the genitive occurs after the NP head, *beṭe* 'sons', which is itself marked with the ergative case. The fact that (6b) is ungrammatical is a clear indication that the genitive phrases cannot be right-adjoined to the NP head.

(6) a. [[nadya=ke   do
Nadya.F.SG=GEN.M.PL two
beṭe]NP=ne]KP gari=ko
son.M.PL=ERG car.F.SG=ACC
cala-yi   hɛ
drive-PERF.F.SG be.PRES.3.SG

'Nadya's two sons have driven the car.

b. * [do beṭe
two son.M.PL
nadya=ke]NP=ne]KP
Nadya.F.SG=GEN.M.PL=ERG
gari=ko   cala-yi
car.F.SG=ACC drive-PERF.F.SG
hɛ
be.PRES.3.SG

The Hindi/Urdu genitive has a wide functional distribution: it appears on adjuncts and nominal arguments. The LFG analysis of Sulger (to appear) is assumed here, which argues for a differentiated treatment of the genitive KP in terms of the

grammatical functions (GF) subject/SUBJ (7a), object/OBJ (7b) and adjunct/ADJUNCT (7c).[4]

(7) a. ram=ki   tɪppani
Ram.M.SG=GEN.F.SG comment.F.SG
'Ram's comment/criticism'

b. gari=ki   tabahi
car.F.SG=GEN.F.SG destruction.F.SG
'the car's destruction'

c. sʊrx rang=ki   mez
red   color.M.SG=GEN.F.SG table.F.SG
'the table of red color'

3 Genitive Scrambling

In addition to the variable word order inside NPs, there are examples showing that the genitive modifiers can occur outside of the NPs they modify. I will refer to this as *Genitive Scrambling*. In (8a), the genitive occurs in the canonical position inside the NP to the left of the head noun. In (8b), the genitive is scrambled outside of the subject NP to the end of the clause; still, it must be analyzed as a modifier of the head noun *dost* 'friend', since it cannot be argued to be an argument of the intransitive verb *a* 'come'.

(8) a. ram=ka
Ram.M.SG=GEN.M.SG
dost   ay-a
friend.M.SG.NOM come-PERF.M.SG
'Ram's friend came.'   (Butt and Zinsmeister, 2009)

b. dost   ay-a
friend.M.SG.NOM come-PERF.M.SG
ram=ka
Ram.M.SG=GEN.M.SG
'Ram's friend came.'   (Butt and Zinsmeister, 2009)

In (9a), the object *gari* 'car' is modified by the genitive *us=ki* 'her/his/its'. The genitive can be

____

[4]Due to space limitations, I do not go into detail regarding the treatment in Sulger (to appear). I will say, however, that the evidence includes binding of a reflexive pronoun as well as iterativity/optionality of nominal arguments vs. adjuncts. Note also that semantically, the genitive may realize various roles as a modifier, e.g., an agent in (7a), a patient in (7b), and an attribute in (7c). This semantic variety is known from many languages, including English; a semantic classification of the genitive is certainly not within the scope of this paper.

scrambled out of the object to the beginning of the clause as in (9b). From the morphosyntax, it is clear that in (9b) the feminine-inflected *ʊs=ki* 'her/his/its' modifies *gaṛi* 'car', since that is the only feminine nominal in the sentence. A very similar example is in (10).

(9) a. ram=ne
         Ram.M.SG=ERG
         ʊs=ki
         PRON.3.SG.OBL=GEN.F.SG
         gaṛi   bazar=mẽ
         car.F.SG.NOM market.M.SG=LOC.IN
         dekʰ-i
         see-PERF.F.SG
         'Ram saw her/his car in the market.'
         (adapted from Bögel and Butt (2013), p.
         301)

     b. ʊs=ki
         PRON.3.SG.OBL=GEN.F.SG
         ram=ne   gaṛi
         Ram.M.SG=ERG car.F.SG.NOM
         bazar=mẽ   dekʰ-i
         market.M.SG=LOC.IN see-PERF.F.SG
         'His/her car, Ram saw in the market.'
         (adapted from Bögel and Butt (2013), p.
         301)

(10) a. tʊm=ne   kɪs=ki
          you=ERG who.SG.OBL=GEN.F.SG
          kɪtab   xɑrid-i?
          book.F.SG.NOM buy-PERF.F.SG
          'Whose book did you buy?' (adapted
          from Bögel and Butt (2013), p. 301)

      b. kɪs=ki   tʊm=ne
          who.SG.OBL=GEN.F.SG you=ERG
          kɪtab   xɑrid-i?
          book.F.SG.NOM buy-PERF.F.SG
          'Whose book did you buy?' (adapted
          from Bögel and Butt (2013), p. 301)

Genitives may also be scrambled to the right. In (11a), a permutation of (9a), the object is topicalized to the front of the clause. In (11b), the genitive phrase modifying the object is scrambled to the right and occurs after the subject. A similar example is given in (12), where *kɪs=ki* 'whose' modifies *kɪtab* 'book', but is not in the same constituent.

(11) a. ʊs=ki
          PRON.3.SG.OBL=GEN.F.SG
          gaṛi   ram=ne
          car.F.SG.NOM Ram.M.SG=ERG
          bazar=mẽ   dekʰ-i
          market.M.SG=LOC.IN see-PERF.F.SG
          'His/her car, Ram saw in the market.'
          (adapted from Bögel and Butt (2013), p.
          301)

      b. gaṛi   ram=ne
          car.F.SG.NOM Ram.M.SG=ERG
          ʊs=ki
          PRON.3.SG.OBL=GEN.F.SG
          bazar=mẽ   dekʰ-i
          market.M.SG=LOC.IN see-PERF.F.SG
          'His/her car, Ram saw in the market.'
          (adapted from Bögel and Butt (2013), p.
          301)

(12) a. kɪs=ki
          who.SG.OBL=GEN.F.SG
          kɪtab   tʊm=ne
          book.F.SG.NOM you=ERG
          xɑrid-i?
          buy-PERF.F.SG
          'Whose book did you buy?' (adapted
          from Bögel and Butt (2013), p. 301)

      b. kɪtab   tʊm=ne
          book.F.SG.NOM you=ERG
          kɪs=ki
          who.SG.OBL=GEN.F.SG
          xɑrid-i?
          buy-PERF.F.SG
          'Whose book did you buy?' (Bögel and
          Butt (2013), p. 301)

Recall that the order within NPs is head-final. As seen in (11)–(12), however, when genitives are scrambled outside of their NP, this order is not necessarily preserved. Using the terminology of Fanselow and Féry (2006), I refer to scrambled genitives that occur before their heads in the sentence as *non-inverted* scrambled genitives, and to scrambled genitives that occur after their heads as *inverted* scrambled genitives.

It is a reasonable assumption that scrambling of genitive phrases is possible since the genitive displays rich morphology which agrees with its head, enabling speakers to identify the nominal in the sentence modified by the genitive. Fanselow and Féry (2006) identify agreement inside NPs as a main factor influencing the availability of discontinuous NPs across languages, but there are also counter-examples against this generalization; Turkish, for example, has discontinuous NPs, in spite of the absence of agreement inside nominal projections.

4 Some Preferences and Constraints

The operation of genitive scrambling does not occur without constraints. This section sums up these constraints, which serve as the empirical background for the XLE implementation of genitive scrambling as described in §5. Each of the constraints was verified by intensive consultation with at least three native speakers.

4.1 Local Attachments are Preferred

Consider (13a), which involves a topicalized object. The possessor of that object can be scrambled to the right as in (13b). In cases such as (13b), *ʊs=ki* is either a scrambled genitive modifying *gaṛi* 'car' or a canonical genitive locally attached to *bag* 'park'; the agreement morphology does not rule out either. Where the agreement morphology permits both scrambled as well as locally attached genitives, local attachments are highly preferred. Here, informants judge *ʊs=ki* 'his/her' as modifying *bag* 'park', but acknowledge that it may also modify *gaṛi* 'car'.

(13) a. ʊs=ki
        PRON.3.SG.OBL=GEN.F.SG
        gaṛi   nadya=ne
        car.F.SG.NOM Nadya.F.SG=ERG
        bag=mẽ   dekʰ-i
        park.F.SG=LOC.IN see-PERF.F.SG
        'Her/his car, Nadya saw in the park.'

    b. gaṛi   nadya=ne
        car.F.SG.NOM Nadya.F.SG=ERG
        ʊs=ki
        PRON.3.SG.OBL=GEN.F.SG
        bag=mẽ   dekʰ-i
        park.F.SG=LOC.IN see-PERF.F.SG
        'The car, Nadya saw in her park.'
        preferred over
        'His/her car, Nadya saw in the park.'

The preference for local attachment is reflected in a principle well-known from cognitive science, first discussed by Kimball (1973) as the *Right Association* principle, and reformulated by Gibson (1991) as the *Recency Preference*.

4.2 Scrambling and Case

The examples above involve genitives that are scrambled out of bare NPs. Genitives may also be scrambled out of NPs that are overtly case-marked; in this case, inverted scrambled genitives are ungrammatical, and the genitive has to precede its head in the clause. Examples are shown in (14). In both sentences, *ram=ke* 'Ram's' modifies *bacco=ne* 'children=ERG', but since the latter is ergative-marked, the former has to precede it.

(14) a. ram=ke   kɑl
        Ram.M.SG=GEN.M.SG.OBL yesterday
        bacco=ne   yɪh
        child.M.PL.OBL=ERG this
        gana   ga-ya
        song.M.SG.NOM sing-PERF.M.SG
        tʰ-a
        be.PAST-M.SG
        'Ram's children sang this song yesterday.'

    b. * bacco=ne   kɑl
        child.M.PL.OBL=ERG yesterday
        ram=ke   yɪh
        Ram.M.SG=GEN.M.SG.OBL this
        gana   ga-ya
        song.M.SG.NOM sing-PERF.M.SG
        tʰ-a
        be.PAST-M.SG

A similar example involving a genitive scrambled from an overtly-marked object NP is given in (15): *ram=ke* 'Ram's' needs to precede its head *kʊṭṭe=ko* 'dog=ACC'.

(15) a. bacco=ne
        child.M.PL.OBL=ERG
        ram=ke   kɑl
        Ram.M.SG=GEN.M.SG.OBL yesterday
        kʊṭṭe=ko   dekʰ-a
        dog.M.SG.OBL=ACC see-PERF.M.SG
        'The children saw Ram's dog yesterday.'

b. * bɑcco=ne
child.M.PL.OBL=ERG
kʊ̣ṭṭe=ko   kɑl
dog.M.SG.OBL=ACC yesterday
ram=ke
Ram.M.SG=GEN.M.SG.OBL
dekʰ-a
see-PERF.M.SG

Recall that genitive KPs modifying nominals in overtly case-marked KPs need to have oblique nominal morphology. One might assume, then, that examples such as (15b) are bad simply because there are several options for the genitive KP to modify a nominal, given the high amount of syncretism in genitive case marking for the oblique; e.g., in (15b) the genitive could modify both *bacco* and *kuṭṭe*. (16) shows that this cannot be the issue. Here, the genitive can modify both nominals, being in linear precedence to both of them; cf. also (14b), which is ungrammatical, even though the agreement morphology clearly rules out any other possibilities of modification aside of *bacco*.

(16) ram=ke   kɑl
      Ram.M.SG=GEN.M.SG.OBL yesterday
      bɑcco=ne   kʊ̣ṭṭe=ko
      child.M.PL.OBL=ERG dog.M.SG.OBL=ACC
      dekʰ-a
      see-PERF.M.SG
      'The children saw Ram's dog yesterday.'
      or
      'Ram's children saw the dog yesterday.'

4.3 Scrambling from Complement Clauses

Another constraint concerns complement clauses. None of my informants judge possessors scrambled out of finite complement clauses as grammatical; cf. the ungrammatical examples in (17). However, a majority of my informants indicate that it is grammatical to scramble genitive phrases from within non-finite complement clauses, e.g., the clause headed by the modal verb *sak* 'can' in (18). This is in line with the findings by Mahajan (1990), Kidwai (1999) as well as Kidwai (2000), who state that scrambling of arguments from within finite complement clauses is generally not accepted, whereas scrambling from infinite complement clauses is.

(17) * ʊs=ki
      PRON.3.SG.OBL=GEN.F.SG
      ram=ne   kɑh-a   kɪh
      Ram.M.SG=ERG say-PERF.M.SG that
      [nina=ne   gaṛi
      Nina.F.SG=ERG car.F.SG.NOM
      dekʰ-i]
      see-PERF.F.SG

(18) ʊs=ki
      PRON.3.SG.OBL=GEN.F.SG
      ram   gaṛi   dekʰ
      Ram.M.SG.NOM car.F.SG.NOM see
      sɑk-a
      can-PERF.M.SG
      'His/her car, Ram could see.'

4.4 No Scrambling out of Adjuncts

The third constraint concerning genitive scrambling is that genitive KPs may not be scrambled from within adjuncts. In (19a), *ʊs=ki* 'her/his/its' is a genitive phrase modifying *bag* 'park', which itself is locative case-marked and an adjunct to the overall clause. It is found that the possessor may not be scrambled from its NP to any other position in the clause (19b–c).

(19) a. ram=ne
          Ram.M.SG=ERG
          ʊs=ki
          PRON.3.SG.OBL=GEN.F.SG
          bag=mẽ   hatʰi
          park.F.SG=LOC.IN elephant.M.SG.NOM
          dekʰ-a
          see-PERF.F.SG
          'Ram saw an elephant in my park.'
      b. * ʊs=ki ram=ne bag=mẽ haṭʰi dekʰ-a
      c. * ram=ne bag=mẽ haṭʰi ʊs=ki dekʰ-a

Island behavior, i.e., the unavailability of constituents for movement/scrambling, is symptomatic for clausal adjuncts and is well-known throughout the literature, first discussed by Ross (1967). It is also a well-known diagnostic for distinguishing arguments from adjuncts, as discussed by, e.g., Needham and Toivonen (2011) in an LFG setting.

4.5 No Scrambling from Deep Within

The last constraint to be discussed here indicates that it is not possible to scramble genitive phrases that are selected by nominals further down a path of grammatical functions. Consider the examples in (20a). *ʃɔhar* 'husband' is modified by a genitive SUBJ *orat=ke* 'the woman's'. *ʃɔhar=ki*, in turn, is an extrinsic possessor SUBJ modifying the overall object of the clause, *gaɽi* 'car'. The structure is as indicated by the bracketing in (20b). In the similar example (21), *sʊrx rang=ke* 'of red color' is an AD-JUNCT modifying *makan* 'house'.

(20) a. ram=ne
     Ram.M.SG=ERG
     orat=ke
     woman.F.SG=GEN.M.SG.OBL
     ʃɔhar=ki
     husband.M.SG=GEN.F.SG
     gaɽi   dek^h-i
     car.F.SG.NOM see-PERF.F.SG
     'Ram saw the woman's husband's car.'

    b. ram=ne [[[orat=ke]$_{SUBJ}$ ʃɔhar=ki]$_{SUBJ}$
      gaɽi]$_{OBJ}$ dek^h-i

(21) a. nina=ne   sʊrx
     Nina.F.SG=ERG red
     rang=ke
     color.M.SG=GEN.M.SG
     makan=ka   darvaza
     house.M.SG=GEN.M.SG door.M.SG
     dek^h-a
     see-PERF.M.SG
     'Nina saw the red house's door.'

    b. nina=ne   [[[sʊrx   rang=ke]$_{ADJUNCT}$
      makan=ka]$_{SUBJ}$ darvaza]$_{OBJ}$ dek^h-a

Given such situations, consider the examples in (22)–(23). In (22a–b), *orat=ke* 'the woman's', the SUBJ genitive KP modifying *ʃɔhar* 'husband', cannot appear outside of the NP it is embedded in, i.e., outside the NP headed by *gaɽi* 'car', since it is embedded too far down in that NP, its GF path being (↑ OBJ SUBJ SUBJ) (starting from the main clause). (23a–b) show that the same restriction holds for attributive genitives such as *sʊrx rang=ke* 'of red color', which has the path (↑ OBJ SUBJ ADJUNCT) here.

(22) a. * orat=ke ram=ne ʃɔhar=ki gaɽi dek^h-i

    b. * ram=ne ʃɔhar=ki gaɽi orat=ke dek^h-i

(23) a. * sʊrx rang=ke nina=ne makan=ka
      darvaza dek^h-a

    b. * nina=ne makan=ka darvaza sʊrx
      rang=ke dek^h-a

5 XLE Implementation

This section describes the implementation of the Hindi/Urdu genitive as well as its scrambling properties and resulting discontinuities. The implementation uses the XLE grammar development platform, which includes an industrial-strength parser and generator for LFG grammars (Crouch et al., 2015).

5.1 General Setup

The lexical entry for the feminine genitive case marker *ki* is given in (24). Recall the agreement pattern of the genitive case marker in Table 1; in XLE, constraining equations can account for the requirements concerning gender, number as well as morphological form. In (24), the constraints are in the form of inside-out constraining equations, since the genitive KP may either be embedded in a SUBJ, ADJUNCT or in an OBJ f-structure inside the head noun's f-structure. The last line in (24) states that the case marker needs to be inside an f-structure that has the feature NTYPE; this ensure that the genitive only occurs as a nominal case (i.e., not on verbal arguments/adjuncts).

```
(24)  kI   K * (^ CASE) =c gen
          (({SUBJ|OBJ|ADJUNCT} ^) GEND) =c fem
          (({SUBJ|OBJ|ADJUNCT} ^) NTYPE).
```

The XLE grammar rules in (25) construct the KP and NP. (25a) states that the KP consists of an NP and an optional case marker K. (25b) states that an NP may consist of a simple pronoun or a modified noun (Nadj). In (25b), the use of the shuffle operator (,), separating the KP, AP and N nodes ensures that each of these nodes may occur in any order, thereby allowing for different word orders inside the NP. The annotation ! <h ^ (making use of the head precedence operator <h) indicates that the currently annotated c-structure node (here: KP or AP) has to precede the c-structure node of the higher-level f-structure, modeling the fact that genitives and other NP modifiers have to precede their

heads. Sample c- and f-structures for (2a) are shown in Figures 1 and 2.[5]

(25) a. `KP --> NP`
          `        (K).`
      b. `NP --> {PRON`
          `       |Nadj}.`
      c. `Nadj = KP*: (! CASE) = gen`
          `            ! <h ^`
          `            {@SUBJ|@OBJ|@ADJUNCT}`
          `      ,`
          `      AP*: @ADJUNCT`
          `           ! <h ^`
          `      ,`
          `      N.`

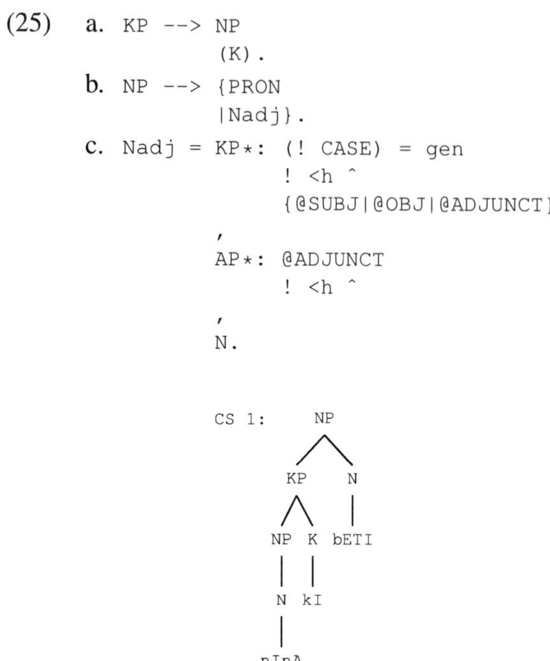

Figure 1: Hindi/Urdu NP c-structure for (2a)

Figure 2: Hindi/Urdu NP f-structure for (2a)

5.2 Generalizing and Implementing Genitive Scrambling

The genitive scrambling facts can be formalized via a functional uncertainty path as in (26).[6] The expression is matched by a variety of paths, e.g., `SUBJ`, `OBJ`, `XCOMP SUBJ`, etc. (`XCOMP` is the grammatical function used for non-finite complement clauses). Thus, (26) describes exactly those paths that scrambled genitives may be extracted from; it does not allow for genitives scrambled from adjuncts, finite complement clauses (which are inside the `COMP` GF) or from deeper GF paths (e.g., `OBJ SUBJ`).

(26) `KP-SCRAMBLE-PATH = (XCOMP)`
      `     {SUBJ|OBJ|OBL|OBJ-GO|OBJ-TH}.`

(27) is the XLE rule template that adds scrambled genitive KPs to the c-structure tree. Functionally, they are annotated as subjects, objects or adjuncts (lines 6–8) inside a path variable instantiated from `KP-SCRAMBLE-PATH` (line 2). Lines 3–5 check the case feature of the head noun; it is either nominative (i.e., a bear NP), in which case there is no precedence constraint, or it is not nominative (i.e., it is overtly case-marked), in which case the genitive is required to precede its head (again implemented using head precedence, see above). Finally, line 9 adds an O(ptimality)T(heory) mark to the scrambled genitive, called `attach`, which marks the analysis as non-optimal when it is in direct competition with a local attachment analysis (which does not carry the OT mark).

(27) `KP-SCRAMBLE = KP*: (! CASE) = gen`
      `    (^ KP-SCRAMBLE-PATH) = %PATH`
      `    { (%PATH CASE) =c nom`
      `    | (%PATH CASE) ~= nom`
      `      ! <h %PATH}`
      `    { (%PATH SUBJ) = !`
      `    | (%PATH OBJ) = !`
      `    |! $ (%PATH ADJUNCT)`
      `    @(OT-MARK attach).`

5.3 Testsuite Creation

To perform regression tests on the implementation, a separate testsuite file was created with examples of vanilla genitives as well as instances of genitive scrambling. The testsuite currently includes 36 grammatical and ungrammatical examples, each between two and eight words long, and has been manually constructed in close collaboration with the native speakers. All grammatical sentences are parsed successfully, while all ungrammatical sentences are ruled out.[7]

---

[5]The rules in the grammar are more complicated than shown here; e.g., the `Nadj` rule includes further nodes such as quantifiers, demonstratives etc. The scheme used by the Hindi/Urdu ParGram grammar for transliterating the Urdu Arabic script is described in Malik et al. (2010) as well as Bögel (2012).

[6]Documentation for the implementation of functional uncertainty in XLE is at `http://ling.uni-konstanz.de/pages/xle/doc/notations.html#N4.1.5`.

[7]One ungrammatical sentence in fact times out with the default XLE timeout setting of 30 seconds, pending investigation.

Given the ambiguity of the genitive discussed in Section 2, all sentences yield ambiguous parse results. As an example, reconsider (13b). The sentence is part of the testsuite and yields two optimal as well as two unoptimal solutions. Under the two optimal readings, *us=ki* 'his/her' locally modifies *bag* 'park' as a subject or an adjunct; under the two unoptimal readings, *us=ki* 'his/her' is a scrambled genitive subject or adjunct modifying *gaṛi* 'car'.

XLE does not display unoptimal solutions by default; the developer/annotator can select the unoptimal solution(s) by clicking the OT mark that controls the (dis)preference. Figure 3 shows the optimal solution where *us=ki* 'his/her' is a subject, while Figure 4 shows the corresponding unoptimal solution, i.e., the scrambled genitive analysis.[8]

```
"gARI nAdiyah nE us kI bAG mEN dEkHI"

      PRED    'dEkH<[23:nAdiyah], [1:gARI]>'
              PRED     'nAdiyah'
              NTYPE    NSEM [PROPER [PROPER-TYPE name]]
      SUBJ             NSYN proper
              SEM-PROP [SPECIFIC +]
           23 ANIM +, CASE erg, GEND fem, NUM sg, PERS 3
              PRED  'gARI'
      OBJ     NTYPE NSEM [COMMON count]
                    NSYN common
            1 CASE nom, GEND fem, NUM sg, PERS 3
                      PRED     'bAG<[45:vuh]>'
                              PRED  'vuh'
                      SUBJ    NTYPE [NSYN pronoun]
                           45 CASE gen, NUM sg, PERS 3, PRON-TYPE pers
      ADJUNCT         NTYPE NSEM [COMMON count]
                            NSYN common
                      SEM-PROP [LOCATION in]
                   77 CASE loc, GEND fem, NUM sg, PERS 3
      LEX-SEM [AGENTIVE +]
      TNS-ASP [ASPECT perf, MOOD indicative]
   104 CLAUSE-TYPE decl, PASSIVE -, VTYPE main
```

Figure 3: Hindi/Urdu NP f-structure for (13b)

```
"gARI nAdiyah nE us kI bAG mEN dEkHI"

      PRED    'dEkH<[23:nAdiyah], [1:gARI]>'
              PRED     'nAdiyah'
              NTYPE    NSEM [PROPER [PROPER-TYPE name]]
      SUBJ             NSYN proper
              SEM-PROP [SPECIFIC +]
           23 ANIM +, CASE erg, GEND fem, NUM sg, PERS 3
              PRED     'gARI<[45:vuh]>'
                       PRED  'vuh'
              SUBJ     NTYPE [NSYN pronoun]
      OBJ          45  CASE gen, NUM sg, PERS 3, PRON-TYPE pers
              NTYPE    NSEM [COMMON count]
                       NSYN common
            1 CASE nom, GEND fem, NUM sg, PERS 3
                      PRED     'bAG'
      ADJUNCT         NTYPE NSEM [COMMON count]
                            NSYN common
                      SEM-PROP [LOCATION in]
                   77 CASE loc, GEND fem, NUM sg, PERS 3
      LEX-SEM [AGENTIVE +]
      TNS-ASP [ASPECT perf, MOOD indicative]
   104 CLAUSE-TYPE decl, PASSIVE -, VTYPE main
```

Figure 4: Hindi/Urdu NP f-structure for (13b)

Future theoretical work includes a comparison with other morphologically-rich languages. An initial investigation has shown that scrambling data in Turkish, as discussed by e.g. Kornfilt (2003), are similar, but display a constraint called the "barrier constraint" by Chomsky (1986), which rules out possessors that occur directly right-adjoined to arguments; the constraint does not exist in Hindi/Urdu. Since ParGram includes a Turkish grammar (Çetinoglu, 2009), a comparison of the annotations necessary to cover the genitive scrambling facts would be interesting.

Acknowledgments

This work is supported by a Nuance Foundation grant on *Tense and Aspect in Multilingual Semantic Construction*. I would like to thank the native speakers who have provided me with judgments; in alphabetical order, these are Qaiser Abbas, Tafseer Ahmed, Rajesh Bhatt, Miriam Butt, Farhat Jabeen, Asad Mustafa, Ghulam Raza and Ashwini Vaidya.

References

Rajesh Bhatt, Bhuvana Narasimhan, Martha Palmer, Owen Rambow, Dipti Misra Sharma, and Fei Xia. 2009. A Multi-Representational and Multi-Layered Treebank for Hindi/Urdu. In *Proceedings of the Third Linguistic Annotation Workshop*, pages 186–189, Sun-

---

[8]The c-structures are not shown here due to space limitations. In the c-structure corresponding to the f-structure in Figure 3, the genitive attaches below the NP headed by *bag* 'park', while in the c-structure for Figure 4, the genitive attaches to the clausal node, resulting in a flat structure.

tec, Singapore, August. Association for Computational Linguistics.

Tina Bögel and Miriam Butt. 2013. Possessive Clitics and Ezafe in Urdu. In Kersti Börjars, David Denison, and Alan Scott, editors, *Morphosyntactic Categories and the Expression of Possession*, pages 291–322. John Benjamins.

Tina Bögel, Miriam Butt, Annette Hautli, and Sebastian Sulger. 2009. Urdu and the Modular Architecture of ParGram. In *Proceedings of the Conference on Language and Technology 2009 (CLT09)*. Center for Research in Urdu Language Processing (CRULP).

Tina Bögel. 2012. Urdu – Roman Transliteration via Finite State Transducers. In *Proceedings of FSMNLP'12*, pages 25–29.

Miriam Butt and Tracy Holloway King. 2004. The Status of Case. In Veneeta Dayal and Anoop Kumar Mahajan, editors, *Clause Structure in South Asian Languages*, pages 153–198. Kluwer.

Miriam Butt and Tracy Holloway King. 2007. Urdu in a Parallel Grammar Development Environment. *Language Resources and Evaluation: Special Issue on Asian Language Processing: State of the Art Resources and Processing*, 41:191–207.

Miriam Butt and Heike Zinsmeister. 2009. ESSLLI 2009 Course on Case, Scrambling and Default Word Order. Course material.

Miriam Butt, Helge Dyvik, Tracy Holloway King, Hiroshi Masuichi, and Christian Rohrer. 2002. The Parallel Grammar Project. In *Proceedings of the COLING-2002 Workshop on Grammar Engineering and Evaluation*, pages 1–7.

Miriam Butt. 1995. *The Structure of Complex Predicates in Urdu*. Dissertations in Linguistics. CSLI Publications.

Özlem Çetinoglu. 2009. *A Large Scale LFG Grammar for Turkish*. Ph.D. thesis, Sabanci University.

Noam Chomsky. 1986. *Barriers*. MIT Press.

Dick Crouch, Mary Dalrymple, Ronald M. Kaplan, Tracy Holloway King, John T. Maxwell III, and Paula Newman, 2015. *XLE Documentation*. Palo Alto Research Center.

Mary Dalrymple. 2001. *Lexical Functional Grammar*, volume 34 of *Syntax and Semantics*. Academic Press, New York.

Gisbert Fanselow and Caroline Féry. 2006. Prosodic and Morphosyntactic Aspects of Discontinuous Noun Phrases: a Comparative Perspective. Manuscript, University of Potsdam.

Edward Gibson. 1991. *A Computational Theory of Human Linguistic Processing: Memory Limitations and Processing Breakdown*. Ph.D. thesis, Carnegie Mellon University, Pittsburgh, PA.

Ayesha Kidwai. 1999. Word Order and Focus Positions in Universal Grammar. In Georges Rebuschi and Laurice Tuller, editors, *The Grammar of Focus*, pages 213–244. John Benjamins.

Ayesha Kidwai. 2000. *XP-Adjunction in Universal Grammar: Scrambling and Binding in Hindi-Urdu*. Oxford University Press.

John Kimball. 1973. Seven Principles of Surface Structure Parsing in Natural Language. *Cognition*, 2:15–47.

Jaklin Kornfilt. 2003. Scrambling, Subscrambling, and Case in Turkish. In Simin Karimi, editor, *Word Order and Scrambling*. Blackwell Publishing.

Anoop Kumar Mahajan. 1990. *The A/A-Bar Distinction and Movement Theory*. Ph.D. thesis, MIT.

Muhammad Kamran Malik, Tafseer Ahmed, Sebastian Sulger, Tina Bögel, Atif Gulzar, Ghulam Raza, Sarmad Hussain, and Miriam Butt. 2010. Transliterating Urdu for a Broad-Coverage Urdu/Hindi LFG Grammar. In *Proceedings of the Seventh Conference on International Language Resources and Evaluation (LREC 2010)*, pages 2921–2927.

Tara Mohanan. 1994. *Argument Structure in Hindi*. Dissertations in Linguistics. CSLI Publications.

Stephanie Needham and Ida Toivonen. 2011. Derived Arguments. In Miriam Butt and Tracy Holloway King, editors, *Proceedings of the LFG11 Conference*, pages 401–421. CSLI Publications.

John Robert Ross. 1967. *Constraints on Variables in Syntax*. Ph.D. thesis, MIT.

Sebastian Sulger, Miriam Butt, Tracy Holloway King, Paul Meurer, Tibor Laczkó, György Rákosi, Cheikh Bamba Dione, Helge Dyvik, Victoria Rosén, Koenraad De Smedt, Agnieszka Patejuk, Özlem Çetinoglu, I Wayan Arka, and Meladel Mistica. 2013. ParGramBank: The ParGram Parallel Treebank. In *Proceedings of the 51st Annual Meeting of the Association for Computational Linguistics (Volume 1: Long Papers)*, pages 550–560, Sofia, Bulgaria, August. Association for Computational Linguistics.

Sebastian Sulger. to appear. *Modeling Nominal Predications in Hindi/Urdu*. Ph.D. thesis, University of Konstanz.

Discontinuous parsing with continuous trees

Wolfgang Maier and **Timm Lichte**
Institute for Language and Information
University of Düsseldorf
Universitätsstr. 1, 40225 Düsseldorf, Germany
`{maierwo,lichte}@phil.hhu.de`

Abstract

We introduce a new method for incremental shift-reduce parsing of discontinuous constituency trees, based on the fact that discontinuous trees can be transformed into continuous trees by changing the order of the terminal nodes. It allows for a clean formulation of different oracles, leads to faster parsers and provides better results. Our best system achieves an F_1 of 80.02 on TIGER.

1 Introduction

Certain structures in natural language can be described as *discontinuous*, in the sense that they consist of two or more parts which are not adjacent. In linguistics, such structures are typically considered the result of some kind of movement of an element out of a "base" position. Discontinuous structures occur across many other languages (Huck and Ojeda, 1987). Sentence (1) is a German example, taken from the NeGra treebank.

(1)   Darüber muss nachgedacht   werden
        Thereof must thought-about be
        'We have to think about that'

In this sentence, the adverb *Darüber*, modifier of the participle *nachgedacht*, is moved to the front. Treebank annotation generally accounts for such structures: Either, the base position of an element is marked with a trace node which is coindexed with the moved element, as it is done, e.g., in the Penn Treebank; or, all parts of a discontinuous constituent are grouped under a single node, as it is done in the

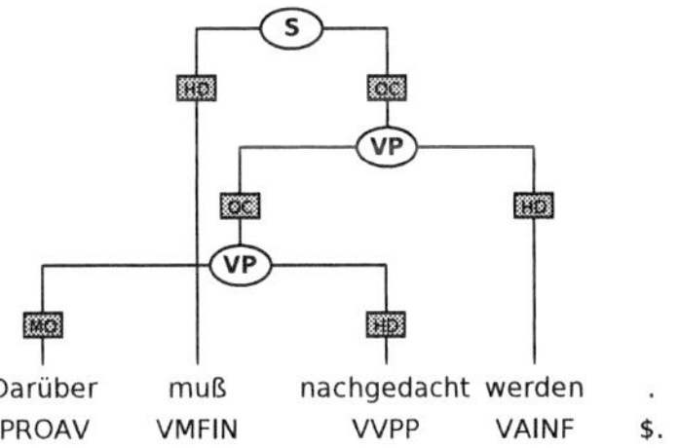

Figure 1: Discontinuous annotation of (1)

German TIGER and NeGra treebanks. This can be seen in Fig. 1, which shows the treebank annotation of (1). The connection between *Darüber* and its reference participle *nachgedacht* is made by grouping both words under a single VP node.

Parsing discontinuous constituents is a challenge, since approaches that produce context-free derivations cannot be used. For treebanks in which discontinuities are represented by traces, various approaches have been presented, mostly based on the extension of a CFG parser with a pre-, post- or in-processing step. See, e.g., Johnson (2002), Dienes and Dubey (2003), Levy and Manning (2004), Schmid (2006), and Cai et al. (2011). For the direct parsing of discontinuous constituents, grammar-based techniques have been used, mostly on the basis of Linear Context-Free Rewriting System (LCFRS) (Vijay-Shanker et al., 1987). LCFRS is an extension of Context-Free Grammar in which a single non-terminal can span $k \geq 1$ continuous parts of the input string; i.e., CFG is a special case of LCFRS in which $k = 1$. See, e.g., Kallmeyer and Maier (2013), van Cranenburgh (2012), Angelov and Ljunglöf (2014), Nederhof and Vogler (2014),

47

Proceedings of DiscoNLP 2016, pages 47–57,
San Diego, California, June 17, 2016. ©2016 Association for Computational Linguistics

or Cohen and Gildea (2015). Even with advanced approaches such as the latter, the high parsing complexity with such approaches is a major bottleneck which tends to lead to low parsing speeds.

Another approach consists of creating a reversible conversion of discontinuous constituents to dependencies, and to parse those with an appropriate dependency parser. This very successful approach is taken by Hall and Nivre (2008) and Fernández-González and Martins (2015).

Recently, Versley (2014) and Maier (2015) have exploited a strategy known from non-projective dependency parsing (Nivre, 2009; Nivre et al., 2009): One can convert every non-projective dependency tree into a projective one by reordering its words. Non-projective dependency parsing can therefore be cast as projective dependency parsing with an additional online reordering operation which allows for the input to be processed out-of-order ("swap"). The same holds for the parsing of discontinuous constituency trees. While Versley (2014) adapts the "easy-first" strategy of Goldberg and Elhadad (2010) to work with a swap operation, Maier (2015) extends the shift-reduce approach of Zhu et al. (2013) correspondingly. Note that the idea of processing linear precedence and immediate dominance for discontinuous parsing separately has also been explored in a grammar-based context by Nederhof and Vogler (2014).

In this paper, we build on the work of Maier (2015) and make two contributions. Firstly, we introduce a new parser transition SKIPSHIFT-i which in comparison to the swap operation reduces the amount of decisions required to be taken in order to produce a discontinuous constituent and therefore leads to fewer errors. Secondly, we address the problem that when processing the input terminals out-of-order, the same tree can be mapped to different parser transition sequences. We introduce an algorithm which reorders the terminals of a tree off-line such that the resulting tree is continuous. The reordered terminals are used as a basis for obtaining an oracle that maps the tree to a canonical transition sequence. All new techniques are implemented within *uparse*, the publicly available parser of Maier (2015).[1] An experimental evaluation shows that

<hr>

[1]https://github.com/wmaier/uparse.

choosing the appropriate terminal order is crucial to parsing success: We obtain state-of-the-art results for discontinuous shift-reduce constituency parsing, namely 80.02 on the TIGER data set of Hall and Nivre (2008).

The remainder of the article is organized as follows. In Sec. 2, we present the basic architecture for shift-reduce parsing with discontinuous constituents of Maier (2015), on which we build our work. Sec. 3 presents our methodology. In Sec. 4, we present our experiments and discuss the results, and Sec. 5 closes the article.

2 Discontinuous Shift-Reduce Parsing

2.1 Basic parser architecture

We base our work on the shift-reduce parser architecture of Maier (2015), which in turn is based on the architecture of Zhu et al. (2013).

As usual in shift-reduce parsing, a parser *state* represents a (partial) derivation. It is a tuple consisting of a *queue* of incoming pairs of input tokens and POS tags[2] which have not yet been processed, and a stack which holds completed constituents. The *initial* parser state has an empty stack and a queue which holds the input string to be parsed. From a given state, other states can be reached via the following state transitions.

- SHIFT shifts a single element from the queue onto the stack.

- BINL-X, resp. BINR-X build a new X constituent with the first two stack elements as its children and its head coming from its left, resp. right child. The new constituent replaces the first two stack elements.

- UNARY-X builds a new X constituent with the first stack element as its child. The new constituent replaces the first stack element.

- SWAP-i handles discontinuous constituents. It allows for a block of i elements from the stack

<hr>

[2]POS tagging and constituency shift-reduce parsing can be done jointly, as demonstrated, e.g., by Mi and Huang (2015). However, note that throughout, we assume POS tagging to be done outside of the parser as in earlier work (Zhu et al., 2013; Maier, 2015).

to be swapped back on the queue, starting with the second stack element.[3]

- FINISH pops the last remaining element from the stack, given that it is labeled with the root label and the queue is empty.

- IDLE can be applied any number of times after FINISH. This compensates for different lengths of analyses (Zhu et al., 2013).

A parser state to which FINISH has been applied is a *final* state. Transitions can only be applied on states which fulfill certain conditions. For instance, SHIFT can only be applied if there are elements left on the queue. The full set of the corresponding conditions is listed in the appendix of Zhang and Clark (2009), and in Maier (2015) (for SWAP).

2.2 Oracles

An *oracle* is used to obtain canonical transition sequences from gold treebank trees. These sequences can then be learned by the parser.

Since we only use transitions that handle unary and binary nodes, incoming trees must be binarized. As in previous work, we use head-outward binarization with binary top and bottom productions, and a single binarization label @X for all X constituents. For details on the binarization, see Maier (2015) and references therein.

For continuous parsing, i.e., when no discontinuous trees have to be handled such as in Zhu et al. (2013), one can use a simple oracle which traverses the tree top-down in postorder. Before the traversal starts, a single IDLE followed by a single FINISH transition are generated. Then, at each binary X node, a corresponding BINL-X / BINR-X is generated; each unary X node leads to a UNARY-X transition. For a terminal, SHIFT is generated. In a last step the transition sequence is reversed.

Discontinuous trees can be handled with the SWAP-*i* transition, which allows for the input to be processed out-of-order (Maier, 2015). The corresponding oracle traverses a treebank tree bottom up left-to-right. Mirroring the parser, it maintains an incoming list of token/POS-pairs to be processed

(initially filled with the sequence of terminals/pre-terminals of the tree), a stack structure holding subtrees of the treebank tree to be processed (initially empty), and a list holding the result.

While the incoming list is not empty, repeat the following two steps.

1. If the stack is not empty, repeat:

   - If the root of the first subtree on the stack is the only child of its parent node p (labeled X), pop the subtree from the stack and push the subtree the root of which is p, then add an UNARY-X transition to the result.
   - If the first two subtrees on the stack share the same parent node p (labeled X), pop both subtrees from the stack and push the subtree the root of which is p, then add a BINR-X / BINL-X transition, depending on the head side of p.

   If no transitions have been added, go to the next step.

2. If the incoming list is not empty, process the next terminal as follows. Determine the leftmost terminal dominated by the right child of the parent of the top element on the stack. If there is no gap, then this is the first element in our incoming list. We can add a single SHIFT, remove the first element from the incoming list and add it to the stack. If there is a gap, then there are $i \geq 1$ terminals between the head of the list and the terminal to be shifted. We therefore add $i+1$ SHIFT and one SWAP-i transition; then we remove the $i+1$st element from the incoming list and add it to the stack.

Note that in the continuous case, both oracles yield the same result. As an example, consider Fig. 1. At the start, no reduce transitions can be added because the stack is empty. We pass to step 2, add a SHIFT transition to the result and remove the first token (*Darüber*) from the list. Then, we must jump over the gap, i.e., we determine the leftmost terminal dominated by the right child of the parent of the topmost stack element. The parent of the topmost stack element is VP, and its rightmost child *nachgedacht*, resp. VVPP. We therefore

---

[3]This operation is called COMPOUNDSWAP$_i$ in Maier (2015); we do not use single SWAP here.

add two SHIFTs and one SWAP-1. This then allows for the addition of a BINR-VP. In the following, we have to jump over *muß* again. The parent of the topmost stack element is (the upper) VP and its rightmost child is *werden*. Therefore, we add again two SHIFTs and one SWAP-1 followed by BINR-VP. Last, we SHIFT the remaining *muss* and add BINR-S.

2.3 Structured prediction

For structured prediction, each parser state is assigned a score. The score of the start state is 0, and the score of the $i + 1$th state is the sum of the score of the ith state and the dot product of a local feature vector obtained through a feature function ϕ and a global weight vector θ. We train θ with the averaged Perceptron using max violation (Huang et al., 2012). Decoding is done with beam search. The beam of size n is initialized with the start state. Then repeatedly, a candidate list is filled with all states which can be built using transitions on states on the beam. The highest scoring n of them are put back on the beam. Parsing is finished if the highest scoring state on the beam is a final state.

2.4 Features

The feature function ϕ works by applying templates to parser states. The templates describe particular configurations of stack and queue. As does Maier (2015), we use the feature template set from Zhang and Clark (2009) as a baseline, and furthermore experiment with the extended features of Zhu et al. (2013). We also use the features for discontinuities from Maier (2015). For the full template list, consult Appendix A.

3 Methodology

We now present the main contributions of this paper, namely, the tree reordering algorithm, the new parser transition, and the new oracles.

3.1 Discontinuous Trees

First, we define the structures which are manipulated by the tree reordering algorithm. A *discontinuous tree* is a directed acyclic graph $T = (V, E, r)$ where V is a set of nodes with $r \in V$ the *root* node, and $E : V \times V$ a set of edges with E^* the reflexive transitive closure of E. For all $v \in V \setminus \{r\}$,

there is exactly one $(u, v) \in E$ with $u \in V$; u is thereby called the *parent* of v and v a *child* of u. Nodes with no children are called *terminals*. We let $V_T = \{v \in V \mid v \text{ is a terminal}\}$; all $v_t \in V_T$ are uniquely numbered from 1 to $|V_T|$ by a function *ind* (Maier and Lichte, 2011). The *yield* of a node $v \in V$ is the set of all terminals it dominates, i.e., for all $v \in V$, $yield(v) = \{u \in V_T \mid (v, u) \in E^*\}$. V is equipped with an order $\prec$, which orders the nodes according to the lowest index of the terminals they dominate. I.e., $u \prec v$ iff $\min(\{ind(u') \mid u' \in yield(u)\}) < \min(\{ind(v') \mid v' \in yield(v)\})$ where $u, v \in V$. We write $c(v)$ for the ordered list of the children of a given node v; for the ith child of v, we write $c(v)[i]$.

Any node $v \in V$ is *discontinuous* (as opposed to *continuous*) if there are $v_1, v_2 \in yield(v)$ such that $ind(v_1) + 1 < ind(v_2)$ and $ind(v_1) + 1 \notin \{ind(v') \mid v' \in yield(v)\}$. If $\{i \mid v_1 < i < v_2\} \cap ind(v) = \emptyset$, then the tuple (v_1, v_2) is called a *gap* of size $ind(v_2) - ind(v_1) - 1$; v_1 and v_2 are called its left and right *border*. T is discontinuous if V contains discontinuous nodes. A continuous node which has discontinuous children is called a *gap creator*.

3.2 Continuous Tree Reordering

As already observed in previous literature (Nivre, 2009; Versley, 2014; Maier, 2015), a discontinuous tree can be made continuous by changing the order of the terminals. The new terminal order must be such that all gaps in yields are eliminated, i.e., it must ensure that discontinuous parts are joined.

In other words, given a tree (V, E, r) we want to produce a function ind_σ to replace ind. ind_σ must be such that all $v \in V$ are continuous. In general, more than one such function will exists for a tree. As an example, consider again the tree in Fig. 1. Two possible permutations of the terminals which eliminate the VP gap would be: *Darüber nachgedacht werden muß* (i.e., $ind_\sigma(\text{Darüber}) = 1$, $ind_\sigma(\text{nachgedacht}) = 2$, $ind_\sigma(\text{werden}) = 3$, $ind_\sigma(\text{muß}) = 4$) and *muß Darüber nachgedacht werden* (i.e., $ind_\sigma(\text{muß}) = 1$, $ind_\sigma(\text{Darüber}) = 2$, $ind_\sigma(\text{nachgedacht}) = 3$, $ind_\sigma(\text{werden}) = 4$). Note that the first order is the complementizer-free order of embedded sentences. The second order is also an acceptable German sentence, namely, the question form of the original sentence.

Given a binarized tree $T = (V, E, r)$, we can obtain different variants of ind_σ systematically with a recursive top-down procedure $reorder$, to be called on r. $reorder$ yields a bijection σ of the set $\{ind(v_t) \mid v_t \in yield(r)\}$ to itself, and we define ind_σ such that for all $v_t \in yield(r)$, $ind_\sigma(v_t) = \sigma(ind(v_t))$. Note that we use tuple notation with angled brackets for the output of the bijection; $\oplus$ denotes tuple concatenation

When called on a node $v \in V$, $reorder$ distinguishes three cases. (1) If v is a terminal, $reorder(v)$ simply yields $[ind(v)]$. (2) If v is an unary node, $reorder(v)$ yields $reorder(c(v)[0])$. (3) If v is a binary node, then there are two different possibilities. $reorder$ can yield $reorder(c(v)[0]) \oplus reorder(c(v)[1])$ or $reorder(c(v)[1]) \oplus reorder(c(v)[0])$. The former is called *left* reordering, since all terminals of the left child are placed in front of all terminals of the right child. Correspondingly, the latter is called the *right* reordering. Not all nodes have to be reordered in the same way; we therefore explore the following reordering selections.

- LEFT: always select left reordering.

- RIGHT: always select right reordering. This also reorders continuous nodes.

- RIGHTD: select right reordering if node is a gap creator, otherwise do not reorder.

- DISTi: select right reordering if node is a gap creator and the left or right child have a gap of size $\geq i$, otherwise do not reorder.

- LABEL: specify a reordering direction for particular labels, and a default reordering for all others.

As an example, let us look at the result of RIGHTD when applied on the tree in Fig. 1. The original set of indices of the root node is $\{1, 2, 3, 4\}$. Since S is binary and a gap creator (S is continuous, but its VP child is discontinuous), we select the right reordering, i.e., $reorder(S)$ is $reorder(\text{muß}) \oplus reorder(\text{VP})$. $reorder(\text{muß})$ is $[2]$. The VP is not a gap creator, i.e., we apply the left reordering and obtain $reorder(\text{VP}) \oplus reorder(\text{werden})$. $reorder(\text{werden})$ is $[4]$. The lower VP is also no gap creator, therefore we apply again the left reordering and obtain $reorder(\text{Darüber}) \oplus reorder(\text{nachgedacht})$. $reorder(\text{Darüber})$ is $[1]$, and $reorder(\text{nachgedacht})$ is $[3]$, i.e., the result for the lower VP is $[1, 3]$. The result for the upper VP is $[1, 3, 4]$, and the result for S is $[2, 1, 3, 4]$. In other words, we obtain $ind_\sigma(\text{Darüber}) = 2$, $ind_\sigma(\text{muss}) = 1$, $ind_\sigma(\text{nachgedacht}) = 3$, and $ind_\sigma(\text{werden}) = 4$, the above mentioned question ordering of the sentence.

3.3 From Swap to Skip-Shift

We introduce a new transition SKIPSHIFT-i, which shifts the ith element from the queue (counting from 0). In other words, it allows the parser to directly skip elements on the queue while shifting. SKIPSHIFT-i underlies the same restrictions as the "regular" SHIFT transition (Zhang and Clark, 2009): The queue must not be empty and the state must not be a final state. Furthermore, if last transition was of type BINR- and led to an intermediate constituent, SKIPSHIFT-i is disallowed.

The new transition reduces the amount of transitions needed to parse a discontinuity. As an example, consider the transition sequence which would be extracted from the tree in Fig. 1 with SHIFT and SWAP, namely SHIFT, SHIFT, SHIFT, SWAP, BINR-VP, SHIFT, SHIFT, SWAP, BINR-VP, SHIFT, BINR-S. Note that the word *muss* is shifted two times and swapped back on the queue before it is finally used in a reduce transition the third time it is shifted. With SKIPSHIFT-i, only 7 instead of 11 decisions are required: SKIPSHIFT-0, SKIPSHIFT-1, BINL-VP, SKIPSHIFT-1, BINL-VP, SKIPSHIFT-0, BINR-S.

3.4 From reordering to oracles

In the case of discontinuities, the bottom-up oracle from Maier (2015) determines the next terminal to be shifted by skipping over the discontinuity through a traversal of the relevant part of the input tree, namely, the path from the left to right border of a gap.

We modify the old oracle such that the order of operations is determined by the terminal reordering obtained with the *reorder* procedure described in Sec. 3.2. If the incoming terminal list is ordered by

ind_σ, the gap borders in the original ordering are joined together. Therefore, no tree walk is necessary to determine the next terminal to be shifted (i.e., the right border of the gap). It is always the first one in the reordered list. We must, however, determine how many terminals have to be shifted and swapped, resp. skipped, relative to the original order, i.e., the size i of the gap that is skipped. For this, we determine the index of the first terminal in the list of terminals to be processed, and then count the number of terminals in the list that have a lower index; i is set to this number minus one. Once determined, i can be used with either SHIFT and SWAP, or with SKIP-SHIFT. With the former, we generate $i + 1$ SHIFT followed by one SWAP-i transition. With the latter, we just generate a single SKIPSHIFT-i transition.

3.5 More features

The new SKIPSHIFT-i operation can access any element in the input queue, not just the first one. In order to make the corresponding information available to the parser, we introduce a new feature set which consist of all token/POS pairs remaining on the queue ("full queue features").

Furthermore, we adapt *swap importance weighting* from Maier (2015). During training, all updates that concern a swap transition are counted twice. We do the same for SKIPSHIFT-i.

4 Experiments

We implement the tree transformations with the corresponding oracles, as well as the SKIPSHIFT-i operation within `uparse`, the publicly available implementation of the parser of Maier (2015).[4]

4.1 Data and Setup

In order to facilitate a comparison, we use the same data as Maier (2015), we use the TIGER treebank release 2.2 with the splits of Farkas and Schmid (2012) and Hall and Nivre (2008). In the former, the first half of the last 10,000 sentences are used for development and the second half for testing, and the rest is left for training. In the latter, the treebank is split into ten parts, such that sentence i is put into part $i \bmod 10$. The first of those parts is used for testing, the concatenation of the rest for training. As usual,

we attach the material which is not included in the annotation (mainly punctuation) to the tree itself.

We run the training for 20 iterations using beam size 4. Other parameters are indicated later. The results are reported as labeled bracket scores, as obtained with the evaluation module of `discodop`.[5] We use the `proper.prm` file of the `discodop` distribution, i.e., root nodes are not included, but punctuation is included in the evaluation.

4.2 Results

All experimental results are listed in Tab. 1 (evaluation on all constituents) and Tab. 2 (evaluation only on discontinuous constituents).

As a baseline, we run a single experiment with the SWAP-i transition. Then, with different settings, we run experiments with the SKIPSHIFT-i transition, using the LEFT, RIGHTD, RIGHT, LABEL, and the DISTi reorderings, choosing 2, 4, and 8 as distance for the latter. For the label-based reordering, we employ the left reordering for all NP and PP nodes, and RIGHTD for all other nodes. NPs and PPs are very similar in the TIGER annotation; the only difference between both is the presence of a preposition in PPs, resp. the absence of it in NPs (Maier et al., 2014). Both are often deeply embedded; we therefore presume that recognizing the entire phrase *before* recognizing the material in the gap is more promising.

The results for SWAP-i confirm the results from Maier (2015). With the SKIPSHIFT-i operation, the parser performs consistently better than with SWAP-i. The best result is obtained with DIST2, an F_1 gain of 2.2 over the swap baseline. Unsurprisingly, RIGHT does not perform well due to the fact that it also aggressively reorders nodes which are continuous; it will not be included in the remaining experiments. When evaluating discontinuous constituents only, DIST8 is the most successful setting. This can be explained by the fact that preferring the right reordering in nodes with children that have large gaps means that the i in SKIPSHIFT-i transitions can be maintained lower than with the left reordering. Since SKIPSHIFT-i with a lower i are seen more frequently in training, results improve. LABEL is not that successful, achieving only a slightly higher precision on discontinuous constituents.

---

[4] https://github.com/wmaier/uparse.

[5] https://github.com/andreasvc/discodop.

	Rec.	Prec.	F_1	Exact
SWAP-i	72.80	74.67	73.72	36.27
Baseline				
LEFT	73.94	75.54	74.73	37.37
RIGHTD	75.15	76.77	75.95	37.19
RIGHT	25.61	22.53	23.97	10.68
LABEL	75.14	76.71	75.92	37.28
DIST2	75.13	76.81	75.96	37.19
DIST4	74.98	76.55	75.76	37.19
DIST8	75.18	76.64	75.88	37.56
+ extended features				
LEFT	74.43	75.87	75.14	37.80
RIGHTD	75.58	77.07	76.32	37.86
LABEL	75.24	76.61	75.92	37.41
DIST2	75.70	**77.25**	**76.46**	37.82
DIST4	75.60	77.07	76.33	37.84
DIST8	75.18	76.61	75.89	37.83
+ extended and disco features				
LEFT	74.77	76.10	75.43	37.84
RIGHTD	**75.73**	77.14	76.43	37.13
LABEL	75.65	77.07	76.35	37.38
DIST2	75.57	76.95	76.25	37.69
DIST4	75.63	77.08	76.35	37.52
DIST8	75.39	76.77	76.08	37.72
+ extended and full queue features				
LEFT	74.44	75.96	75.19	**38.54**
RIGHTD	75.42	76.96	76.18	38.20
LABEL	75.30	76.91	76.10	37.90
DIST2	75.65	77.17	76.40	38.01
DIST4	75.43	76.83	76.12	38.22
DIST8	75.20	76.54	75.87	37.95
+ extended features and imp. weighting				
LEFT	74.45	75.82	75.13	37.53
RIGHTD	75.44	76.77	76.10	37.48
LABEL	75.42	76.84	76.12	37.70
DIST2	75.51	76.89	76.19	37.37
DIST4	75.18	76.55	75.86	37.68
DIST8	75.00	76.36	75.67	37.12
+ extended, disco and full queue feature + importance weighting				
LEFT	74.87	76.23	75.54	37.61
RIGHTD	75.28	76.63	75.95	37.03
LABEL	75.30	76.76	76.02	36.94
DIST2	75.43	76.95	76.19	37.54
DIST4	75.33	76.65	75.98	37.05
DIST8	75.16	76.64	75.89	37.28

Table 1: Results (all constituents)

	Rec.	Prec.	F_1	Exact
SWAP-i	10.29	23.64	14.34	8.03
Baseline				
LEFT	14.31	18.64	16.19	12.33
RIGHTD	10.90	25.27	15.24	8.74
RIGHT	1.73	0.18	0.33	0.51
LABEL	10.58	25.88	15.02	8.75
DIST2	11.82	28.15	16.64	9.73
DIST4	11.63	25.40	15.96	10.10
DIST8	13.53	27.11	18.05	11.29
+ extended features				
LEFT	13.54	21.38	16.58	12.20
RIGHTD	10.25	31.00	15.41	9.04
LABEL	10.19	27.92	14.94	8.99
DIST2	11.02	31.32	16.31	9.99
DIST4	11.22	29.16	16.20	10.25
DIST8	11.78	26.00	16.21	10.56
+ extended and disco features				
LEFT	**14.90**	29.53	19.80	14.17
RIGHTD	8.43	42.13	14.05	8.14
LABEL	8.87	45.91	14.86	8.57
DIST2	9.03	41.49	14.83	9.43
DIST4	10.14	42.86	16.40	9.62
DIST8	11.42	37.96	17.55	11.06
+ extended and full queue features				
LEFT	14.30	24.86	18.16	12.98
RIGHTD	10.96	30.69	16.15	9.79
LABEL	11.12	29.02	16.08	9.57
DIST2	11.58	31.93	17.00	9.91
DIST4	11.03	27.74	15.78	9.81
DIST8	12.06	27.60	16.79	10.42
+ extended features and imp. weighting				
LEFT	13.39	24.24	17.25	12.36
RIGHTD	9.15	31.98	14.23	7.79
LABEL	9.47	33.83	14.80	8.32
DIST2	10.00	33.59	15.41	9.12
DIST4	9.70	32.50	14.94	9.41
DIST8	10.54	29.14	15.48	9.78
+ extended, disco and full queue feature + importance weighting				
LEFT	14.31	35.27	**20.36**	**13.80**
RIGHTD	8.91	**45.93**	14.92	8.37
LABEL	8.39	43.10	14.04	8.44
DIST2	8.45	42.62	14.11	8.67
DIST4	8.91	41.11	14.65	8.72
DIST8	10.95	41.84	17.35	10.55

Table 2: Results (discontinuous constituents)

	V	M	**here**	vC	H&N	F&M
F_1	74.23	79.52	80.02	79.00	79.93	**85.53**
E	37.32	44.32	45.11	41.33	37.78	**51.21**

Table 3: Results for sentence length ≤ 40 on H&N data

The fact that we need less operations in total in order to build a tree (in comparison to SWAP-i) is reflected in reduced parsing times. With SWAP-i, we need 63 seconds to parse the entire test set (79.5 sent./sec.), with SKIPSHIFT-i and LEFT, we only need 49 seconds (101.8 sent./sec.).

When adding the extended features from Zhu et al. (2013), the trend seen in Maier (2015) is repeated: Looking deeper into the structures on the stack leads to a higher performance when looking at all constituents. On discontinuous constituents, we obtain a improved precision, but a slightly worse recall. The features for discontinuities have also the same effect as in Maier (2015), no improvement is achieved on all constituents. The precision on discontinuous constituents is, however, much higher while the corresponding recall drops sharply, indicating data sparseness. Adding the full queue features to the extended features only has a very small effect.

Also, adding importance weighting alone is not very successful. However, when we combine the extended, the discontinuous and the full queue features with importance weighting, we achieve the best result on discontinuous constituents; surprisingly this happens when using the LEFT reordering.

Last, for comparison, we run experiments on the Hall and Nivre (2008) (H&N) data set. We run our own parser (LEFT; extended, discontinuous, and full queue features; importance weighting); and also `discodop` (van Cranenburgh and Bod, 2013) (vC) (default settings, using gold POS tags). Tab. 3 shows the corresponding results along with those of Versley (2014) (V), Maier (2015) (M), H&N and Fernández-González and Martins (2015) (F&M) (taken from Maier (2015)). Note that we do improve on M, but still lie much behind F&M.

4.3 Discussion

What about the big picture? In spite of an improvement on Maier (2015), the scores on the discontinuous constituents remain very low. A manual analysis of the parsing results leads us to the conclu-sion that the strongest point of discontinuous shift-reduce parsing, namely the locality of the search which leads to its speed, is also its biggest weakness. Certain structures can simply not be recognized almost "by definition". For instance, in order to correctly recognize an NP with an extraposed modifier, the reduction of the full NP must be delayed until the complete modifier has been recognized. With the current parsing model, in some situations, there is just no way of knowing if a delay is necessary, since the modifier can be still out of reach for the feature function when the first part of the full NP has already been recognized. Due to beam search, once the NP is reduced, we cannot backtrack, i.e., the modifier cannot be attached later.

One way of addressing this problem could be the use of exact search, such as in Thang et al. (2015). However, there is another perspective. An important finding of the experiments is that recognizing material in gaps *before* the discontinuous constituent itself (RIGHTD) leads to high precision and low recall on discontinuous constituents, while recognizing the discontinuous constituent first (LEFT) leads to more errors, but also catches more cases (lower precision, higher recall). The reason for this is that in the former case, one decides too late and in the latter case too early if a partially recognized constituent is part of a discontinuous structure. We conjecture that what makes the parsers of Fernández-González and Martins (2015) and van Cranenburgh and Bod (2013) successful are their mechanisms of handling this issue: The former joins the recognition of a terminal with the decision of what part of a (potentially discontinuous) constituent it belongs to. The latter gets structure-global context by building the final tree as a combination of discontinuous base structures. This makes it particularly more successful on discontinuous structures, achieving Prec./Rec./F_1 of 33.77/50.29/40.41 on them (compared to our result of 19.36/39.71/26.03) (unfortunately, Fernández-González and Martins (2015) have not reported results on discontinuous constituents alone). In future work, we will explore possibilities of integrating such a mechanism in a shift-reduce approach.

We have seen that choosing the transition order well, i.e., picking the right oracle, is crucial for parsing success. We therefore want to explore how the order of transitions affects parsing results in the continuous case. A particular transition order could be forced via a tree transformation such as *right-corner transform* (Schuler et al., 2010). Concretely, right-corner transform would give preference to easier transition orders in which we reduce as soon as possible, i.e., long sequences of SHIFTs would be avoided.

Last, it should be noted that the application of SKIPSHIFT-i is not limited to discontinuous constituency parsing. We want to apply our method to non-projective dependency parsing, where SKIPSHIFT-i could be used instead of swap-eager/lazy transitions (Nivre et al., 2009) in a parsing framework such as the one of Zhang and Nivre (2011). This would also allow for an "intersection" between our work and then one of Fernández-González and Martins (2015).

5 Conclusion

We have presented a new tree reordering method which makes discontinuous constituency trees continuous. The reordering method can be used to obtain oracles for discontinuous shift-reduce parsing. In conjunction with a new parser transition, we have achieved state-of-the-art results for discontinuous shift-reduce constituency parsing.

Appendix A. Feature Templates

Our parser uses feature templates from previous work. For the sake of completeness, we list them here. s_i and q_i stand for the ith item on stack and queue, w is the head word, t the head tag and c the constituent label (w, t and c are identical on preterminal level). l and r (ll and rr) are the left and right children (grand-children) of the corresponding element on the stack; u deals with unary constituents.

The following baseline features have been presented by Zhang and Clark (2009).

unigrams

$s_0tc, s_0wc, s_1tc, s_1wc, s_2tc, s_2wc, s_3tc, s_3wc,$
$q_0wt, q_1wt, q_2wt, q_3wt,$
$s_0lwc, s_0rwc, s_0uwc, s_1lwc, s_1rwc, s_1uwc$

bigrams

$s_0ws_1w, s_0ws_1c, s_0cs_1w, s_0cs_1c, s_0wq_0w, s_0wq_0t,$
$s_0cq_0w, s_0cq_0t, s_1wq_0w, s_1wq_0t, s_1cq_0w, s_1cq_0t,$
$q_0wq_1w, q_0wq_1t, q_0tq_1w, q_0tq_1t$

trigrams

$s_0cs_1cs_2w, s_0cs_1cs_2c, s_0cs_1cq_0w, s_0cs_1cq_0t,$
$s_0cs_1wq_0w, s_0cs_1wq_0t, s_0ws_1cs_2c, s_0ws_1cq_0t$

The *extended* features have been introduced by Zhu et al. (2013).

extended

$s_0llwc, s_0lrwc, s_0luwc, s_0rlwc, s_0rrwc,$
$s_0ruwc, s_0ulwc, s_0urwc, s_0uuwc, s_1llwc,$
$s_1lrwc, s_1luwc, s_1rlwc, s_1rrwc, s_1ruwc$

The following *disco* features stem from Maier (2015). As explained there, in the following templates, x denotes the *gap type* of a stack element. It can be "none" (tree on stack is fully continuous), "pass" (there is a gap at the root), and "gap" (the root of this tree fills a gap, i.e., its children have gaps, but the root does not). y stands for the sum of all gap lengths.

unigrams

$s_0xwc, s_1xwc, s_2xwc, s_3xwc,$
$s_0xtc, s_1xwc, s_2xtc, s_3xwc,$
$s_0xy, s_1xy, s_2xy, s_3xy$

bigrams

$s_0xs_1c, s_0xs_1w, s_0xs_1x, s_0ws_1x, s_0cs_1x,$
$s_0xs_2c, s_0xs_2w, s_0xs_2x, s_0ws_2x, s_0cs_2x,$
$s_0ys_1y, s_0ys_2y, s_0xq_0t, s_0xq_0w$

Acknowledgments

We would like to thank Omri Abend for discussions. Thanks also to the three anonymous reviewers for valuable comments and suggestions. This work was partially funded by Deutsche Forschungsgemeinschaft (DFG).

References

Krasimir Angelov and Peter Ljunglöf. 2014. Fast statistical parsing with parallel multiple context-free grammars. In *Proceedings of the 14th Conference of the European Chapter of the Association for Computational Linguistics*, pages 368–376, Gothenburg, Sweden.

Shu Cai, David Chiang, and Yoav Goldberg. 2011. Language-independent parsing with empty elements. In *Proceedings of the 49th Annual Meeting of the Association for Computational Linguistics: Human Language Technologies*, pages 212–216, Portland, OR.

Shay B. Cohen and Daniel Gildea. 2015. Parsing linear-context free rewriting systems with fast matrix multiplication. *CoRR*, abs/1504.08342.

Péter Dienes and Amit Dubey. 2003. Antecedent recovery: Experiments with a trace tagger. In *Proceedings of the 2003 Conference on Empirical Methods in Natural Language Processing*, pages 33–40, Sapporo, Japan.

Richard Farkas and Helmut Schmid. 2012. Forest reranking through subtree ranking. In *Proceedings of the 2012 Joint Conference on Empirical Methods in Natural Language Processing and Computational Natural Language Learning*, pages 1038–1047, Jeju Island, Korea, July. Association for Computational Linguistics.

Daniel Fernández-González and André F. T. Martins. 2015. Parsing as reduction. In *Proceedings of the 53rd Annual Meeting of the Association for Computational Linguistics and Teh 7th International Joint Conference on Natural Language Processing of the Asian Federation of Natural Language Processing*, Beijing, China.

Yoav Goldberg and Michael Elhadad. 2010. An efficient algorithm for easy-first non-directional dependency parsing. In *Human Language Technologies: The 2010 Annual Conference of the North American Chapter of the Association for Computational Linguistics*, pages 742–750, Los Angeles, CA.

Johan Hall and Joakim Nivre. 2008. Parsing discontinuous phrase structure with grammatical functions. In Bengt Nordström and Aarne Ranta, editors, *Advances in Natural Language Processing*, volume 5221 of *Lecture Notes in Computer Science*, pages 169–180. Springer, Gothenburg, Sweden.

Liang Huang, Suphan Fayong, and Yang Guo. 2012. Structured perceptron with inexact search. In *Proceedings of the 2012 Conference of the North American Chapter of the Association for Computational Linguistics: Human Language Technologies*, pages 142–151, Montréal, Canada, June. Association for Computational Linguistics.

Geoffrey Huck and Almerindo Ojeda, editors. 1987. *Discontinuous constituency*. Academic Press, New York.

Mark Johnson. 2002. A simple pattern-matching algorithm for recovering empty nodes and their antecedents. In *Proceedings of the 40th Annual Meeting of the Association for Computational Linguistics*, pages 136–143, Philadelphia, PA.

Laura Kallmeyer and Wolfgang Maier. 2013. Data-driven parsing using probabilistic linear context-free rewriting systems. *Computational Linguistics*, 39(1):87–119.

Roger Levy and Christopher Manning. 2004. Deep dependencies from context-free statistical parsers: Correcting the surface dependency approximation. In *Proceedings of the 42nd Meeting of the Association for Computational Linguistics (ACL'04), Main Volume*, pages 327–334, Barcelona, Spain.

Wolfgang Maier and Timm Lichte. 2011. Characterizing discontinuity in constituent treebanks. In *Formal Grammar. 14th International Conference, FG 2009. Bordeaux, France, July 25-26, 2009. Revised Selected Papers*, volume 5591 of *LNCS/LNAI*, pages 167–182, Berlin, Heidelberg, New York. Springer-Verlag.

Wolfgang Maier, Miriam Kaeshammer, Peter Baumann, and Sandra Kübler. 2014. Discosuite - A parser test suite for German discontinuous structures. In *Proceedings of the Ninth International Conference on Language Resources and Evaluation (LREC'14)*, Reykjavik, Iceland. European Language Resources Association (ELRA).

Wolfgang Maier. 2015. Discontinuous incremental shift-reduce parsing. In *Proceedings of the 53rd Annual Meeting of the Association for Computational Linguistics and the 7th International Joint Conference on Natural Language Processing (Volume 1: Long Papers)*, pages 1202–1212, Beijing, China, July. Association for Computational Linguistics.

Haitao Mi and Liang Huang. 2015. Shift-reduce constituency parsing with dynamic programming and pos tag lattice. In *Proceedings of the 2015 Conference of the North American Chapter of the Association for Computational Linguistics: Human Language Technologies*, pages 1030–1035, Denver, Colorado, May–June. Association for Computational Linguistics.

Mark-Jan Nederhof and Heiko Vogler. 2014. Hybrid grammars for discontinuous parsing. In *Proceedings of COLING 2014, the 25th International Conference on Computation Linguistics: Technical Papers*, pages 1370–1381, Dublin, Ireland.

Joakim Nivre, Marco Kuhlmann, and Johan Hall. 2009. An improved oracle for dependency parsing with online reordering. In *Proceedings of the 11th International Conference on Parsing Technologies (IWPT'09)*, pages 73–76, Paris, France.

Joakim Nivre. 2009. Non-projective dependency parsing in expected linear time. In *Proceedings of the Joint Conference of the 47th Annual Meeting of the ACL and the 4th International Joint Conference on Natural Language Processing of the AFNLP*, pages 351–359, Singapore.

Helmut Schmid. 2006. Trace prediction and recovery with unlexicalized PCFGs and slash features. In *Proceedings of the 21st International Conference on Computational Linguistics and 44th Annual Meeting of the Association for Computational Linguistics*, pages 177–184, Sydney, Australia.

William Schuler, Samir AbdelRahman, Tim Miller, and Lane Schwartz. 2010. Broad-coverage parsing using human-like memory constraints. *Computational Linguistics*, 36(1):1–30.

Le Quang Thang, Hiroshi Noji, and Yusuke Miyao. 2015. Optimal shift-reduce constituent parsing with structured perceptron. In *Proceedings of the 53rd Annual Meeting of the Association for Computational Linguistics and the 7th International Joint Conference on Natural Language Processing (Volume 1: Long Papers)*, pages 1534–1544, Beijing, China, July. Association for Computational Linguistics.

Andreas van Cranenburgh and Rens Bod. 2013. Discontinuous parsing with an efficient and accurate DOP model. In *Proceedings of The 13th International Conference on Parsing Technologies*, Nara, Japan.

Andreas van Cranenburgh. 2012. Efficient parsing with linear context-free rewriting systems. In *Proceedings of the 13th Conference of the European Chapter of the Association for Computational Linguistics*, pages 460–470, Avignon, France.

Yannick Versley. 2014. Experiments with easy-first non-projective constituent parsing. In *Proceedings of the First Joint Workshop on Statistical Parsing of Morphologically Rich Languages and Syntactic Analysis of Non-Canonical Languages*, pages 39–53, Dublin, Ireland.

K. Vijay-Shanker, David Weir, and Aravind K. Joshi. 1987. Characterising structural descriptions used by various formalisms. In *Proceedings of the 25th Annual Meeting of the Association for Computational Linguistics*, pages 104–111, Stanford, CA.

Yue Zhang and Stephen Clark. 2009. Transition-based parsing of the Chinese treebank using a global discriminative model. In *Proceedings of the 11th International Conference on Parsing Technologies (IWPT'09)*, pages 162–171, Paris, France.

Yue Zhang and Joakim Nivre. 2011. Transition-based dependency parsing with rich non-local features. In *Proceedings of the 49th Annual Meeting of the Association for Computational Linguistics: Human Language Technologies*, pages 188–193, Portland, Oregon, USA, June. Association for Computational Linguistics.

Muhua Zhu, Yue Zhang, Wenliang Chen, Min Zhang, and Jingbo Zhu. 2013. Fast and accurate shift-reduce constituent parsing. In *Proceedings of the 51st Annual Meeting of the Association for Computational Linguistics (Volume 1: Long Papers)*, pages 434–443, Sofia, Bulgaria.

Discontinuity (Re)^{2}visited: A Minimalist Approach to Pseudoprojective Constituent Parsing

Yannick Versley
LinkedIn*
yversley@linkedin.com

Abstract

In this paper, we use insights from Minimalist Grammars (Keenan and Stabler, 2003) to argue for a context-free approximation of discontinuous structures that is both easy to parse for state-of-the-art dynamic programming constituent parsers and has a simple and effective method for the reconstruction of discontinuous tree structures.

The results achieved on the Tiger treebank – paired with state-of-the-art constituent parsers such as the BLLIP and Berkeley parsers – both improve on existing transformation-based approaches for representing discontinuous structures and the state-of-the-art results of Fernández-González and Martins' (2015) parsing-as-reduction approach.

1 Introduction

For languages with free(r) word order and richer morphology, predicate-argument structure (dependencies of words and their heads/governors) and topology (contiguous phrases or regions in the sentence) do not always match up. Hence, constituency parsing techniques that rely on a context-free backbone either have to do with a language-dependent approximation that puts topology at the center (e.g. the TüBa-D/Z treebank of Telljohann et al., 2009, based on topological fields) or can only produce an approximation of the actual predicate-argument structures (as is the case with most parsing approaches targeting the Negra and Tiger treebanks, cf. Skut et al., 1997; Brants et al., 2002).

As an alternative to this procrustean choice, practitioners have traditionally preferred dependency

structures, which today offer straightforward ways to deal with nonprojective structures in practical ways despite the fact that exact parsing of nonprojective dependencies with second-order factors is intractable in general (McDonald, 2006).

In the following, we present a principled treatment for approximating discontinuous syntactic structures by context-free ones. The resulting novel technique for pseudoprojective parsing is well suited for lexicalized as well as unlexicalized projective parsers, and yields a feasible solution for accurate probabilistic parsing of discontinuous structures.

2 Related work

Grammar-based approaches to constituent parsing based on minimally context-sensitive formalisms such as LCFRS/MCFG can give guarantees of polynomial-time parsability. However, the step to practical (i.e., fast and accurate) parsing is much larger than is the case for context-free structures: Specifically, binarization is a key to yielding probabilistic formulations with a good tradeoff between expressivity and sparsity e.g. in the parser of Charniak (2000). Binarization, however, is non-straightforward for LCFRS (Gildea, 2010; van Cranenburgh, 2012), and, unlike for CFG, it is ineffective to obtain a grammar with lower parsing complexity. As a result, parsers directly based on LCFRS such as Kallmeyer and Maier (2013) are rather limited in terms of speed and accuracy.

Greedy (and beam-search) parsing of discontinuous constituents has recently seen some progress in the form of approaches that use swapping techniques in transition-based parsing of discontinuous constituents (Versley, 2014; Maier, 2015). A further strain of approaches uses other dependency parsing techniques by reducing discontinuous con-

---

*Work was done at the University of Heidelberg

Proceedings of DiscoNLP 2016, pages 58–69,
San Diego, California, June 17, 2016. ©2016 Association for Computational Linguistics

stituent parsing to a dependency labeling problem (Hall and Nivre, 2008; Fernández-González and Martins, 2015). However, none of these two groups of approaches easily lend themselves to reranking (Collins, 2000; Charniak and Johnson, 2005) or comparable techniques.

As in van Cranenburgh and Bod (2013), we assume that pairing k-best parsing of context-free structures with a deterministic back-transform to discontinuous structures is a feasible approach to yield k-best lists of discontinuous structures. While van Cranenburgh and Bod rely on a complex ranking mechanism as the second step, we show that refinements to the first steps can already yield results that surpass the state of the art without any separate ranking step.

3 Pseudoprojective parsing

After initial successes with head-lexicalized PCFG parsing for English (Collins, 1997; Charniak, 2000), researchers tried to apply these models to languages that show less configurationality than English. For Czech, (Collins et al., 1999) reordered the original word sequence into one where the corresponding tree becomes continuous. For German, (Dubey and Keller, 2003) transform the treebank by raising discontinuous parts to a higher node in the tree.

Both of these approaches will yield parsing models that (potentially) produce sensible trees for feasible sentences that have a continuous syntactic structure (which comprises the large majority of sentences in English, but may only cover less than half of sentences in typical text for German or Czech). As such, these approximations would be problematic for not offering a path from unparsed tokens as they occur in the text to (potentially) discontinuous trees reflecting predicate-argument structure.

Subsequent approaches such as Levy and Manning (2004) use a multiple-step algorithm to revert the changes introduced by node raising by (heuristically or automatically) identifying NULL elements in the tree, and in a second step identifying dislocated material and linking it up with an appropriate NULL position. Unlike work for heuristic reattachment of dependencies such as Hall and Novak (2005) or Nivre and Nilsson (2005), however, this work is relatively complex. Levy and Manning's

evaluation is also performed on the individual steps rather than in a framework that looks at the complete process of parsing and reattachment.

Boyd (2007) proposes an approximation of LCFRS's block structure to get to a tree transformation that is, in difference to a pure node raising approach, reversible. Boyd labels the blocks of a discontinuous nodes by appending a special suffix (i.e. "VP*" instead of "VP"), and later merging these nodes in a top-down fashion. We will discuss this approach in more detail in section 3.2.

Boyd herself compares her approach of block-based transformation to a setting where node raising was applied to the training corpus but no back-transformation was used (similar to parsing models distributed with modern constituent parsers). Undoing the block-based transformation yielded a better result than node-raising without back-transformation using gold part-of-speech tags.

Contra Boyd, Rehbein and van Genabith (2009) find in an evaluation based on f-structure conversion that Boyd's way of transforming trees gives worse results to their approach. Hsu (2010) looks purely at how well parsers are able to reproduce the structures created by pseudoprojective transformations, and finds that parsers introduce more errors in Boyd's method than in the node-raising method.[1]

3.1 Formalizing pseudoprojectivity

For our purposes a tree $T = (\mathrm{NT} \cup \{t_1, \ldots, t_n\}), E)$ over a sequence of terminals Term $= t_1, \ldots, t_n$ is a directed acyclic graph such that (i) terminals have no children (ii) all nonterminal nodes have at least one child, (iii) all nodes have at most one parent and (iv) that there is a unique topmost node that dominates all other nodes. For the nodes of such a tree we can recursively assign a *yield* function such that the yield of t_i is $\{i\}$ and the yield of a nonterminal node is the union of the yields of the children.

We call a node *contiguous* if its yield is a contiguous subsequence; we call a tree contiguous if all its nodes are contiguous.

---

[1] A reviewer points out that these results should be seen in the context of the experimental framework used – Rehbein only uses the Berkeley parser, and Hsu only uses plain unbinarized PCFGs – and that particular transformations may be more or less appropriate for specific parsers.

A **pseudoprojective transform** over a set $\mathcal{T}$ of trees is a pair $(proj, unproj)$ of functions with the following properties:

- *proj* is a total function from trees in $\mathcal{T}$ to trees. For any tree $T \in \mathcal{T}$, the value $proj(T)$ is a projective tree over the same terminal sequence.

- *unproj* is a partial function from projective trees to trees from $\mathcal{T}$. For any $T' \in proj(\mathcal{T})$, $proj(unproj(T')) = T'$

- *proj* (and by extension *unproj*) preserve contiguous nodes: if T contains a node with label a and a contiguous yield $i..j$, $proj(T)$ must contain a node with label a and a contiguous yield $i..j$. If a contiguous node a_1 has a contiguous ancestor a_2, the ancestor relationship between a_1 and a_2 is preserved in $proj(T)$.

- There is a set of *barrier nodes* B among the contiguous nodes from $T \cap T'$, minimally including the topmost node and all terminal nodes. If $proj(T)$ contains a node not contained in T with a ancestor $n^a \in B$ and a descendent $n^d \in B$, then T must contain a noncontiguous node with ancestor n^a and a descendent n^d.

(I.e. $proj(T) = T$ for all contiguous trees).

Note that we do not require *proj* to be injective (in many useful cases it is not), nor do we say anything about *unproj*'s behaviour on trees outside of $proj(\mathcal{T})$. Possibilities for *proj* include simply deleting discontiguous nodes, adjusting their spans by reparenting (as in node raising) and/or adding other nodes.

3.2   LCFRS-inspired approximations

A Linear Context-Free Rewriting System (LCFRS) is a grammar where nodes in the parse tree do not correspond to a single span, but to a fixed number of *blocks*, yielding productions such as

$$S_1(uvwxy) \rightarrow VP_2(u, x)\, V_1(v)\, NP_2(w, y)$$

In grammar-based parsing, the number of blocks (i.e. letter variables in the production rule) determines the parsing complexity; for pseudo-projective transforms, the most important distinction is between (contiguous) blockdegree 1 nodes and (discontiguous) nodes with a larger blockdegree.

Boyd (2007) proposes a pseudoprojective transformation that approximates LCFRS's block structure: Boyd labels the blocks of a discontinuous nodes by appending a special suffix (i.e. "VP*" instead of "VP"), and later merging these nodes in a top-down fashion.

Van Cranenburgh (2012) suggests a refinement of Boyd's approximation – independently disc where the different blocks of a discontinuous phrase receive different labels (yielding an approximate production of S $\rightarrow$ VP*[1] V NP*[1] VP*[2] NP*[2])

In practice, we found that van Cranenburgh's approach creates many rare categories such as VP*[12], and that limiting the numbers in the superscripts yields identical performance to Boyd's approach.

3.3   A new look at node raising

If we have a treebank where a VP is the projection of a verb, we (or the parser) have a concrete expectation of what to find inside a VP node. In contrast, LCFRS and Boyd's transforms treat the trees as non-lexicalized construct: for a VP, we would get two VP ⋆ nodes with rather different properties. The second (in our case) contains a verb and other children that we would normally expect under a VP (not VP*) node, and the first one contains topicalized material. Furthermore, the occurrence of both topicalization and extraposition can mean that there is no strong regularity among "first parts" and "second parts", which renders van Cranenburgh's refinement ineffective.

If we consider trees to have head terminals, and the hierarchical relations inducing dependency relations between terminals (see definition in the appendix), we could hope for **contiguous subtree preservation**, a stronger version of contiguity preservation:

Given two trees T_1 and T_2 where the terminal node subsequences $i_1..j_1$ of T_1 and $i_2..j_2$ of T_2 as well as the dependencies between the terminals in these subsequences are identical. If T_1 has a contiguous subtree with a yield of $i_1..j_1$, then $proj(T_2)$ should also contain the same contiguous subtree.

Node raising (leaving aside unary productions) fulfills this subtree conservation property for treebanks such as Tiger that use sibling adjunction (see Carreras et al., 2008). The LCFRS-derived pseudoprojective transformations do not, which intuitively

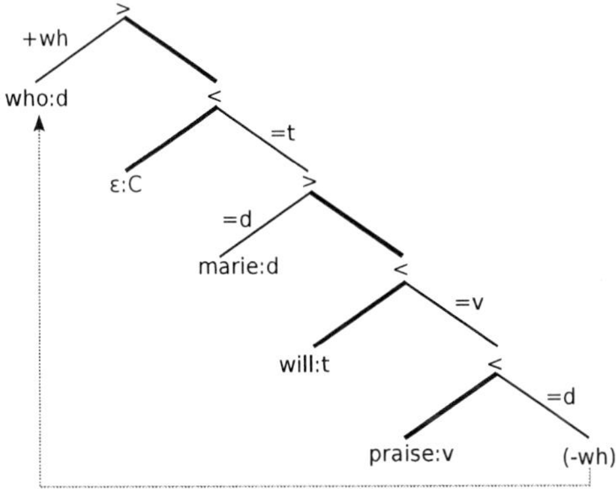

Figure 1: A Minimalist Grammar tree

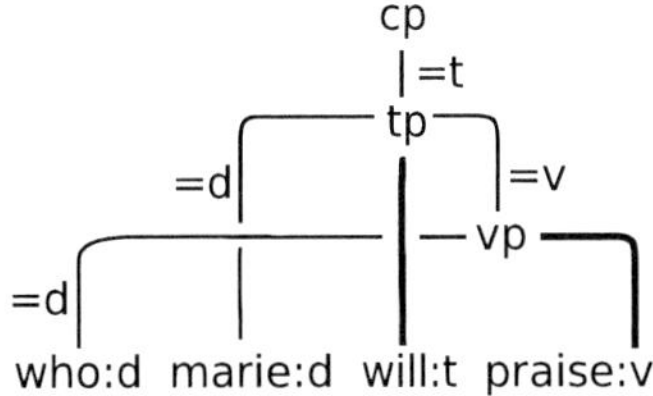

Figure 2: A Tiger-style tree

explains the result of Hsu (2010) that the latter are harder for a context-free parser.

As a conclusion, we see two properties we want to maintain: on the one hand, subtree contiguity preservation seems to be beneficial for getting more accurate parses of the projectivized trees, on the other hand, some marking to aid deprojectivization seems very helpful.

4 Approximating Minimalist Grammars

The approach we present in this paper is based on an approximation of minimalist grammars (MG), stemming from a family of approaches that is popular in mainstream generative linguistics (Chomsky, 1986). Transformational grammar and its descendants have inspired some early work on parsing beyond context-free structures (Dorr, 1987; Lin, 1993), but have for a long time lacked a formalization that would enable more principled work.

Minimalist grammars (in the sense we will use here) are a grammar formalism introduced by Stabler (1997) and Keenan and Stabler (2003) that belongs to the class of *minimally context-sensitive grammars* (Vijay-Shanker et al., 1987; Michaelis, 1998), and carry (in comparison with LCFRS) the benefit of being a lexicalized formalism, and potentially of yielding more compact grammars (Michaelis, 1998) and a more natural model of probability assignments (Hunter and Dyer, 2014).

At the core of Minimalist Grammars are nodes/expressions that carry a category (e.g. x) together with valencies for certain categories (=x, x=) and attractee features (e.g. −w), which designate a node as being moved from its argument position to

a higher node, and attractor features (e.g. +w) which designates a node as a host for moved constituent of the corresponding type. A MOVE operation extracts a $-x$ constituent into a $+x$ position, whereas a MERGE operation adjoins one node to another.

To illustrate the correspondence between the analysis assigned by a minimalist grammar and our target representation (flat discontinuous trees), let us compare Figures 1 and 2: On one hand, MG assumes binary adjunctions while the Tiger annotation scheme has flat phrases – this kind of variation in annotation scheme, while it may influence the structures preferred by PCFG and similar models, is semantically equivalent (Johnson, 1998). On the other hand, the representation with discontinuous phrases eliminates all empty nodes (both the empty complementizer and the trace of the moved *who*), sometimes yielding headless phrases.

We should emphasize here that, while many insights about constraints in movements that are valid in Minimalist Grammars are still valid in actual treebanks (whenever we take care to allow for notational differences), it is not true in general that annotated treebanks are designed using the criteria that are applied in the Minimalist Program (indeed, Minimalist Grammars have the goal of providing a formal grammar to express such ideas in a more theory-neutral way), nor do decisions about headedness, argumenthood, and the modeling of moved nodes necessarily correspond to those that one would make in an MG.

Beyond couching the relation between predicate-argument trees and surface trees in more principled terms (see also Boston et al., 2010 for a discussion of the relation to dependencies), what do we gain?

The Shortest Move Constraint posits that any material that is moved must attach at the first possible host node (i.e., for a moved phrase of type $-x$, attach to the lowest ancestor with the feature $+x$. With the caveat that SMC may not be appropriate for all types of movement (e.g. scrambling), it firstly provides an intuition on possible hosts for dislocated material (whereas the rule of *"raise the nodes up to a host node where the material can be attached without discontinuity"* is of a much more practical nature), while simultaneously predicting that any (potential) host phrase must also act as a barrier for movement.

Following the discussion of Boston et al. (2010), we find a plausible rationale for contiguous subtree preservation. A downside is that undoing *Move*-based dislocation – especially if we consider node raising as the protypical example – would need more information. Consider the following sentence:

(1) *Ich   habe* [np *den   Mann* [pp *mit*
     I have   the man   with the
     dem   Hamster]] *gesehen* [*der grinst*]
     hamster seen   which grins
     I have seen the man with the hamster which grins

In this case, the attachment of the relative clause to *Mann* (man) or to *Hamster* (hamster) is an instance of general attachment ambiguity, and while we can use very general preferences (attach low; prefer attaching as an argument rather than as an adjunct, cf. Hobbs and Bear, 1990), correct attachment often requires semantic or context-dependent information. (LCFRS-inspired transforms pass this problem onto the parser, in a form that poorly fits state-of-the-art parsing models).

4.1 Representing Moved Phrases

If we look at minimalist grammars from our *pseudoprojective transform* perspective, we see that even when we want a transform that fulfills the *contiguous subtree preservation* criterion (which includes Boyd's and van Cranenburgh's solution, even though they are pseudoprojective transforms in our sense), we can solve the problem differently from – and hopefully better than – node raising.

Marcus et al. (1994) and later Skut et al. (1997), in a solution that we will call the *trace-filler mechanism* try to ensure a relation between host phrase and the argument-structure parent by inserting an empty

node in the latter and coindexing with the dislocated material; empty nodes are not supported by today's parsers, and the idea of encoding the coindexation by appending slash categories to phrases has been shown to be non-beneficial (Schiehlen, 2004).

We can preserve contiguous subtrees and yet want to add some marking, we could insert a phrase between the host phrase and the dislocated material, in the simplest case one single fixed category, as in

(2) [vp [np den Mann [pp mit dem Hamster]] gesehen [X [s der grinst]]]

where we inserted an additional X node between host and dislocated material. In difference to simple node raising, this would encode the information which nodes were dislocated and which ones were not in the tree rather than leaving it implicit.

The **LR** scheme for adding additional information to raised nodes, which we propose here, leaves the block of the sentence that includes its head with an unchanged node label, but labels the other part as being left- or right-dislocated, yielding, in the above example, VP$\star$L, VP and VP$\star$R as labels if the middle phrase contains the head of the VP. In our example, we would obtain the following:

(3) [vp [np den Mann [pp mit dem Hamster]] gesehen [NP*R [s der grinst]]]

Similar to the *trace-filler* view, and different from the LCFRS view, we distinguish between the main part of a phrase (normally the one containing the head) and discontinuous (moved) parts. We mark the moved parts with the concatenation of the original parent label and a $\star$L or $\star$R suffix. In comparison with node raising, the additional node fulfills an important function as it both helps the parser recognize where such moved or extraposed material can occur, based on topology (i.e., outside context) as well as the material itself, and also provides useful information for reattachment.

4.2 Simple Heuristics for Backtransformation

Adopting a minimalist perspective on reattachment, we would assume that a parser for context-free structures can plausibly produce the *derived structures* that capture sentence topology but not necessarily the full set of argument and adjunct dependencies.

method	F_1
uncross, no reattach	94.99
LR + top-down reattach	97.90
LR + bottom-up reattach	99.20
+S barrier	99.08

Table 1: Heuristic reattachment: roundtrip results on Tiger sentences 40475-45474

To capture the discontinuous structures, we investigate two reattachment heuristics:

- The **top-down** heuristic chooses an appropriate node from the siblings of the dislocated phrase, similar to the way that Boyd's or van Cranenburgh's reattachment algorithm would operate.

- The **bottom-up** heuristic iterates over the yield of the parent node (limited either to the part left of the dislocated one for $*R$ ones, otherwise the part right of it), to produce a sequence of all suitable descendents of the parent node in a close-to-far, low-to-high fashion.

Evidence from reconstructing gold data (see table 1) shows that the *bottom-up* heuristic is more accurate in the reconstruction, which is consistent with the preference on low attachment as formulated by, e.g., Hobbs and Bear (1990).

Considering the relation to Minimalist Grammar and the Shortest Move Constraint, we would expect that certain nodes act as **barriers** and can block dislocation or movement across them: In example (4) (see figure 3), such a barrier constraint would prevent the fronted subclause *"nehmen die Überlegungen Gestalt an"* (if the plans become more concrete) to the VP internal to the relative clause instead of the VP of the matrix sentence.

In our experiments with projectivising the development set of the Tiger treebank and subsequently reattaching dislocated phrases (see table 1), we see that top-down reattachment already provides a 60% error reduction with respect to simply leaving nodes unattached, and that using a preference for lower attachment (*"bottom-up reattach"*) yields a further 60% error reduction in terms of phrase F_1. In contrast, we see that having sentence (S) nodes block movement leads to a slight decrease in accuracy.

5 Experimental set-up

In the following parsing experiments, we want to compare more directly the accuracy of our **LR** scheme of projectivization and reattachment to that of, e.g. Boyd's proposal while taking into account many of the concerns that occur in practical parsing today, in particular the compatibility with other techniques used to improve parsing accuracy (linguistic tree transformations, products of latent variable grammars, word clustering-based generalizations of words). As we are specifically concerned about the behaviour with more unknown words and different distributions of syntactic constructions that occurs in out-of-domain corpora, we exclusively use the part-of-speech tags assigned by the parsing model itself.

Corpora used As an in-domain corpus that we split into a training, development and testing set, we use the Tiger treebank (Brants et al., 2002), which encodes argument and adjunct relations in a discontinuous constituent structure with edge labels. We use two splits that were used in the literature for parsing experiments: the first, called the *SPMRL split* reproduces the train/development/test portions of Farkas and Schmid (2012) and was used in the SPMRL shared tasks of 2013 for dependency and constituency parsing, using sentences 1–40474 as training set, the next 5000 as development set, and the remaining 5000 as a test set. The second split was first used in the experiments of Hall and Nivre (2008) and uses folds 9 and 10 in a 10-fold setup as development and testing portions, respectively.

As an out-of-domain dataset, we use the Smultron treebanks of Volk et al. (2015), which include portions of a novel (sophie), business reports (economy), texts about mountaineering (alpine) as well as extracts from the manual of a DVD player (dvdman). The annotation of the Smultron treebanks is loosely based on the Tiger scheme but differs in two important respects: on one hand, the Tiger scheme merges PP nodes with the noun phrases that is the argument of the preposition, yielding one single PP phrase; on the other hand, the Smultron annotation scheme uses extra nodes for unary noun, verb and adjective phrases that would be elided in the Tiger scheme. For a sensible comparison, we use a transformed version of the Smultron treebanks where unary nodes are deleted and argu-

(4)   [**VP*L** Nehmen die Überlegungen Gestalt an], würden die Frankfurter,   [**S** die   im Januar
       take   the thoughts   shape on, would   the Frankfurt+ADJ,   which in January
1988 [**VP** ihr   125jähriges Bestehen feiern]   können], [**VP** die Verbindung zu ihren historischen
1988   their 125-year   existence celebrate can,   the connection to their historical
Wurzeln kappen].
roots   clip.
"If the plans become more concrete, the Frankfurt group, which had its 125-year anniversary in
January 1988 would cut the the connection to their historical roots."

Figure 3: An example sentence where the closest VP is not a suitable movement target

ment NPs of prepositional phrases are unwrapped.

Parsing models For reasons of simplicity, we limit ourselves to a small number of generative parsing models that have been shown to work well for context-free parsing.

The **BLLIP parser** (of which we use the generative model only and not the discriminative reranking part) uses a "maximum-entropy-inspired" probabilistic model that produces head-lexicalized constituents from the inside out while conditioning on the two previous neighbours, the grandparent constituents, and their heads (Charniak, 2000).

The **PCFG-LA** parsing model of Petrov et al. (2006) uses a zeroth-order right-markovized version of the treebank which is subsequently augmented with latent symbol refinements in order to improve the fit, using smoothing and a split-merge procedure to avoid overfitting in the EM-based refinement process. We found that four split-merge iterations (instead of the default six) gave the best results with the linguistically transformed trees.

As the PCFG-LA model learns a latent-variable augmentation of the treebank trees and most often reaches a non-unique local maximum of the EM objective, it is possible and useful to combine multiple PCFG-LA models to reach an even better performance using a **product grammar** approach where each rule is scored by a product-of-experts of multiple parsers (Petrov, 2010).

For the out-of-domain parsing, Candito and Seddah (2010) found that replacing words with clusters improved the generalization ability of parsers. After preliminary experiments showed that replacing all words with clusters actually had a negative effect, our setting using **word clusters** only replaces words that occur fewer than five times, using word clusters

derived with the Marlin tool (Müller and Schuetze, 2015) and text from the DECOW corpus[2], limiting the vocabulary size to the most frequent 250 000 word types as done by Müller and Schütze.

Finally, we also include in our investigation the use of **linguistic tree transformations**, which e.g. Dubey (2005) as well as Versley and Rehbein (2009) found useful both for unlexicalized and discriminative PCFG parsing. In particular, we use lowering of parenthetic material as proposed by Maier et al. (2012) to reduce the complexity of discontinuities, but also markers for relative clauses and comparative phrases, linguistically motivated subcategorization information for sentences, added case information to noun phrases, as well as refing part-of-speech classes using some morphological information.

5.1 Comparing Boyd with LR

For each of the three parsers (BLLIP, PCFG-LA, PCFG-LA product grammar) we produce transformed trees with the non-annotated treebank trees (`orig`) as well as the enriched ones (`xform`), using Boyd's projectivization transform (`boyd`) and the one proposed here (`LR`).

Quite expectedly, we find that head-lexicalized parsing using the BLLIP parser is substantially helped by the linguistically motivated tree transformations. Somewhat less intuitively, as the earlier results of Petrov et al. (2006) for English indicate that basic transformations such as head annotation do not help PCFG-LA models, we find that our linguistically motivated transformations substantially help both single PCFG-LA and product grammars. We also see that the LR transform performs slightly worse than Boyd's transform in the BLLIP parser,

---

[2] http://www.corporafromtheweb.org

variant	BLLIP				PCFG-LA				LA-product			
	F1	EX	POS	discF1	F1	EX	POS	discF1	F1	EX	POS	discF1
orig-Boyd	80.32	43.75	97.55	68.41	82.35	42.95	97.63	70.55	83.11	45.66	97.76	72.68
orig-LR	81.28	45.71	97.68	70.02	82.27	43.57	97.71	71.46	83.29	45.81	97.80	72.95
xform-Boyd	82.01	44.67	97.70	71.55	81.35	42.71	97.55	70.92	83.62	46.16	97.72	74.43
xform-LR	81.93	45.27	**97.73**	71.64	82.43	43.49	97.68	72.77	84.18	46.90	**97.84**	75.43
LR + cleanup	82.19	45.53	**97.73**	71.85	82.43	43.49	97.68	72.77	**84.36**	47.08	**97.84**	75.56
LR + filter	**82.20**	**45.63**	97.72	**72.09**	**82.58**	**43.87**	**97.69**	**73.11**	84.09	**47.31**	97.79	**75.81**

Table 2: Comparison on the Tiger development set, sentences with $\leq$ 70 words

whereas the tendency is exactly reversed in PCFG-LA-based parsing. Looking at the evaluation results when ignoring continuous constituents (see table 2, *discF1* columns), we see that the LR scheme specifically improves the quality of discontinuities, sometimes by a slight amount, and sometimes by as much as one percent).

Dealing with invalid solutions Some of the decrease in performance for the BLLIP parser for the LR scheme is due to the occasional dislocated phrases (e.g. NP*R) that cannot be reattached and are then left behind. For the Boyd transform, our implementation already reverts discontinuity-marked phrases (e.g. NP*) to the original label (e.g. NP).

To deal with the 'invalid' phrases, we propose two solutions: the first one, which we call the **cleanup** strategy, involves a post-processing step in which all dislocated phrase nodes are deleted (and their daughters attached to the deleted phrase's parent). The second one, which we call the **filter** strategy, involves producing ranked list of parses, of which we delete any parse that includes dislocated nodes that cannot be reattached. Of the remaining parses, we chose the highest-scoring one.

For the BLLIP parser, we find that both the cleanup step and the kbest list filter result in improvements over the default version, while the advantage of the filtering-based approach over the simpler cleanup approach is very slight at best.

5.2 Comparing with the state of the art

Table 4 compares the result of our pseudoprojective parsing approach to other evaluation results on the Tiger treebank using parser-assigned POS tags.[3]

We find that our BLLIP parsing model already

performs quite well, going beyond the results of van Cranenburgh and Bod (2013) that use a PCFG base parser followed by a DOP-inspired reranking step, or the discriminative parsing results of Versley (2014). Using the product-grammar approach, we find that our approach outperforms the parsing-as-reduction approach of Fernández-González and Martins (2015) by a small margin in the Hall/Nivre split, also yielding much improved (+1.9%) evaluation results for the case of the SPMRL split.

5.3 Experiments with Out-of-domain parsing

Table 3 shows the results on different treebanks from SMULTRON in comparison with those on Tiger. We see that out-of-domain results are substantially lower than those achievable on the Tiger development set: The novel (sophie) performs relatively well while performance on the other domains falls off even more. The most difficulties are due to the DVD manuals (dvdman), which already Seeker and Kuhn (2014) argue to be due to several phenomena not seen in well-edited text.

If we compare the accuracy of the POS assignment from the PCFG-LA parsing models to both the tagging results of Seeker and Kuhn (2014) and our own, in each case using the Marmot CRF tagger Müller et al. (2013), we see that in all cases (except for the Alpine domain) the parser is able to make use of the syntactic context to achieve improved part-of-speech accuracy, even if the overall difficulty of the out-of-domain texts is higher. Use of word clusters seems to be especially helpful in those cases where the parser has difficulty at the POS level.

6 Summary

In this paper, we have presented a new, linguistically well-motivated method for transforming discontinuous trees to context-free ones and back.

---

[3]Fernandez-Gonzalez and Martins report substantially higher results using gold part-of-speech tags.

Parser	LF1/70	EX/70	POS
TIGERDEV			
multi+sm4	84.18	46.90	97.84
multi+sm4+clust	84.31	47.51	97.74
ALPINE			
multi+sm4	74.18	32.70	93.79
multi+sm4+clust	74.80	33.96	93.96
marmot Seeker14			94.42
ECONOMY			
multi+sm4	74.38	22.05	91.73
multi+sm4+clust	74.50	22.44	92.40
marmot Seeker14			91.83
SOPHIE			
multi+sm4	77.71	38.56	96.51
multi+sm4+clust	77.53	38.19	96.41
marmot Seeker14			95.20
DVDMAN			
multi+sm4	71.54	25.78	90.55
multi+sm4+clust	72.45	26.56	90.22
marmot Seeker14			90.81

Table 3: Comparative results for parsing the SMULTRON treebanks (LR without cleanup)

Tiger-H&N (pred)	$L \leq 40$		all	
	F1	EX	F1	EX
Hall&Nivre 2008	75.33	32.63	—	—
van Cranenburgh '13	78.8-	40.8-	—	—
Fernandez&Martins '15	82.57	45.93	81.12	44.48
Ours, BLLIP	81.16	43.17	79.68	41.87
Ours, PCFGLA-prod	82.93	44.26	81.93	42.87
Tiger-SPMRL (pred)	$L \leq 70$		all	
	F1	EX	F1	EX
Versley 2014	73.90	37.00	—	—
Fernandez&Martins '15	77.72	38.75	77.32	38.64
Ours, BLLIP	76.96	35.52	76.52	35.42
Ours, PCFGLA-prod	79.84	39.61	79.50	39.50

Table 4: Test set results on the split of Hall and Nivre (2008) and on the SMPRL split

Because this method allows us to make effective use of state-of-the-art parsing for continuous trees (similar to the parsing-as-reduction approach leveraging state-of-the-art models for dependency parsing), this transformation approach has a substantial advantage over models that use a more complex grammar formalism but have to use a simpler statistical model.

Using three generative probabilistic models, we showed that our method performs better than the older transformation approach of Boyd (2007), and outperforms the current state of the art for discontinuous parsing on the Tiger treebank, the parsing-as-reduction approach of Fernández-González and Martins (2015). Future work will explore feature-based statistical models for reattachment and parse selection.

Acknowledgements The research described in this paper was supported by the Leibniz Society and the Baden Württemberg ministry of science, research and the arts as part of the ScienceCampus *Empirical Linguistics and Computational Natural Language Modeling*. The author is grateful to Jen Sikos and Alexis Palmer, as well as the three anonymous reviewers, for helpful comments on earlier versions of this paper.

References

Boston, M. F., Hale, J. T., and Kuhlmann, M. (2010). Dependency structures derived from Minimalist Grammars. In Ebert, C., Jäger, G., and Michaelis, J., editors, *MOL 10/11*, volume 6149 of *Lecture Notes in Computer Science*, pages 1–12. Springer-Verlag, Berlin Heidelberg.

Boyd, A. (2007). Discontinuity revisited: An improved conversion to context-free representations. In *Proceedings of the Linguistic Annotation Workshop (LAW 2007)*.

Brants, S., Dipper, S., Hansen, S., Lezius, W., and Smith, G. (2002). The TIGER treebank. In *Proc. TLT 2002*.

Candito, M.-H. and Seddah, D. (2010). Parsing word clusters. In *Proceedings of the First Workshop on Statistical Parsing of Morphologically-Rich Languages (SPMRL 2010)*.

Carreras, X., Collins, M., and Koo, T. (2008). TAG, dynamic programming, and the perceptron for efficient, feature-rich parsing. In *Proceedings of CoNLL*.

Charniak, E. (2000). A maximum-entropy-inspired parser. In *Sixth Applied Natural Language Processing Conference (ANLP-NAACL 2000)*.

Charniak, E. and Johnson, M. (2005). Coarse-to-fine n-best parsing and maxent discriminative reranking. In *Proc. ACL 2005*.

Chomsky, N. (1986). *Barriers*. Linguistic Inquiry Monographs. MIT Press.

Collins, M. (1997). Three generative, lexicalized models for statistical parsing. In *Proc. ACL 1997*.

Collins, M. (2000). Discriminative reranking for natural language parsing. In *ICML 2000*.

Collins, M., Hajič, J., Ramshaw, L., and Tillmann, C. (1999). A statistical parser for Czech. In *Proceedings of ACL 1999*.

Dorr, B. J. (1987). Principle-based parsing for machine translation. Technical report, Massachusetts Institute of Technology Artificial Intelligence Laboratory.

Dubey, A. (2005). What to do when lexicalization fails: parsing German with suffix analysis and smoothing. In *ACL-2005*.

Dubey, A. and Keller, F. (2003). Probabilistic parsing for German using sister head dependencies. In *ACL'2003*.

Farkas, R. and Schmid, H. (2012). Forest reranking through subtree ranking. In *EMNLP-CoNLL 2012*.

Fernández-González, D. and Martins, A. F. T. (2015). Parsing as reduction. In *Proceedings of the 53rd Annual Meeting of the Association for Computational Linguistics and the 7th International Joint Conference on Natural Language Processing (Volume 1: Long Papers)*, pages 1523–1533, Beijing, China. Association for Computational Linguistics.

Gildea, D. (2010). Optimal parsing strategies for linear context-free rewriting systems. In *Proceedings of NAACL 2010*.

Hall, J. and Nivre, J. (2008). Parsing discontinuous phrase structure with grammatical functions. In *Proceedings of the 6th International Conference on Natural Language Processing (GoTAL 2008)*.

Hall, K. and Novak, V. (2005). Corrective modeling for non-projective dependency parsing. In *Proceedings of the Ninth International Workshop on Parsing Technology (IWPT 2005)*.

Hobbs, J. R. and Bear, J. (1990). Two principles of parse preference. In *Coling 1990*.

Hsu, Y.-Y. (2010). Comparing conversions of discontinuity in PCFG parsing. In *Proceedings of the Ninth International Workshop on Treebanks and Linguistic Theories*.

Hunter, T. and Dyer, C. (2014). Distributions on minimalist grammar derivations. In *Proceedings of the 13th Meeting on the Mathematics of Language (MoL 13)*.

Johnson, M. (1998). Pcfg models of linguistic tree representations. *Computational Linguistics*, 24(4):613–632.

Kallmeyer, L. and Maier, W. (2013). Data-driven parsing using probabilistic linear context-free rewriting systems. *Computational Linguistics*, 39(1):87–119.

Keenan, E. L. and Stabler, E. P. (2003). *Bare Grammar*. CSLI Publications, Stanford.

Levy, R. and Manning, C. (2004). Deep dependencies from context-free statistical parsers: correcting the surface dependency approximation. In *ACL 2004*.

Lin, D. (1993). Principle-based parsing without overgeneration. In *Proceedings of ACL 1993*.

Maier, W. (2015). Discontinuous incremental shift-reduce parsing. In *Proceedings of the 53rd Annual Meeting of the Association for Computational Linguistics and the 7th International Joint Conference on Natural Language Processing (Volume 1: Long Papers)*, pages 1202–1212, Beijing, China. Association for Computational Linguistics.

Maier, W., Kaeshammer, M., and Kallmeyer, L. (2012). PLCFRS parsing revisited: Restricting the fan-out to two. In *Proceedings of the 11th*

International Workshop on Tree Adjoining Grammar and Related Formalisms (TAG+11).

Marcus, M., Kim, G., Marcinkiewicz, M. A., MacIntyre, R., Bies, A., Ferguson, M., Katz, K., and Schasberger, B. (1994). The Penn treebank: Annotating predicate argument structure. In *Workshop on Human Language Technology*.

McDonald, R. (2006). Online learning of approximate dependency parsing algorithms. In *EACL 2006*.

Michaelis, J. (1998). Derivational minimalism is mildly context-sensitive. In *Logical Aspects of Computational Linguistics*.

Müller, T., Schmid, H., and Schütze, H. (2013). Efficient higher-order CRFs for morphological tagging. In *Proceedings fo EMNLP 2013*.

Müller, T. and Schuetze, H. (2015). Robust morphological tagging with word representations. In *Proceedings of the 2015 Conference of the North American Chapter of the Association for Computational Linguistics: Human Language Technologies*, pages 526–536, Denver, Colorado. Association for Computational Linguistics.

Nivre, J. and Nilsson, J. (2005). Pseudo-projective dependency parsing. In *Proceedings of ACL 2005*.

Petrov, S. (2010). Products of random latent variable grammars. In *HLT-NAACL 2010*.

Petrov, S., Barett, L., Thibaux, R., and Klein, D. (2006). Learning accurate, compact, and interpretable tree annotation. In *COLING-ACL 2006*.

Rehbein, I. and van Genabith, J. (2009). Automatic acquisition of lfg resources for german: As good as it gets. In *Proceedings of LFG09*.

Schiehlen, M. (2004). Annotation strategies for probabilistic parsing in German. In *Proc. Coling 2004*.

Seeker, W. and Kuhn, J. (2014). An out-of-domain test suite for dependency parsing of German. In *Proceedings of LREC 2014*.

Skut, W., Krenn, B., Brants, T., and Uszkoreit, H. (1997). An annotation scheme for free word order languages. In *Proceedings of the Fifth Conference on Applied Natural Language Processing (ANLP-97)*.

Stabler, E. (1997). Derivational minimalism. In *Logical Aspects of Computational Linguistics*, pages 68–95.

Telljohann, H., Hinrichs, E. W., Kübler, S., Zinsmeister, H., and Beck, K. (2009). Stylebook for the Tübingen Treebank of Written German (TüBa-D/Z). Technical report, Seminar für Sprachwissenschaft, Universität Tübingen.

van Cranenburgh, A. (2012). Efficient parsing with linear context-free rewriting systems. In *EACL 2012*.

van Cranenburgh, A. and Bod, R. (2013). Discontinuous parsing with an efficient and accurate DOP model. In *Proceedings of the International Conference on Parsing Technologies (IWPT 2013)*.

Versley, Y. (2014). Experiments with easy-first nonprojective constituent parsing. In *Proceedings of the First Joint Workshop on Statistical Parsing of Morphologically Rich Languages and Syntactic Analysis of Non-Canonical Languages*, pages 39–53, Dublin, Ireland. Dublin City University.

Versley, Y. and Rehbein, I. (2009). Scalable discriminative parsing for German. In *Proc. IWPT 2009*.

Vijay-Shanker, K., Weir, D. J., and Joshi, A. K. (1987). Characterizing structural descriptions produced by various grammatical formalisms. In *Proceedings of the 25th Annual Meeting of the Association for Computational Linguistics (ACL 1987)*.

Volk, M., Göhring, A., Rios, A., Marek, T., and Samuelsson, Y. (2015). SMULTRON (version 4.0) — The Stockholm MULtilingual parallel TReebank. An English-French-German-Quechua-Spanish-Swedish parallel treebank with sub-sentential alignments.

Appendix A. Notational clarifications

For two trees T and T' covering the same sequence of terminals, and containing no unary productions, we define the **intersection tree** $T \cap T'$ as follows:

- If we identify nonterminals with (label, yield) pairs, the nonterminals of $T \cap T'$ are exactly those (label, yield) pairs that correspond to nonterminals of both T and T'.

- The set of edges of $T \cap T'$ is determined as the cover relation of its descendent relation. A node n_1 is a descendent of a node n_2 iff $\mathrm{yield}(n_1) \subseteq \mathrm{yield}(n_2)$.

We can extend this definition to trees containing unary productions if we consider mappings L_T from yields to label sequences (i.e., $\mathcal{P}(\mathbb{N}_n) \to \Sigma^*$ if Σ is our set of labels).

We can define this mapping for a tree as follows:

- if there is no node in T with a yield y, then $L_T(y) = \varepsilon$

- if T contains one or more nodes with the same yield, they form a chain of unary productions. Given the sequence $l_1, \ldots l_m \in \Sigma^*$ of the labels of this sequence (read from top to bottom), we then set $L_T(y) = l1, \ldots, l_m$.

Taking (e.g.) the longest common prefix of two such sequences gives us an operation that is idempotent, commutative and associative.

If we identify nonterminals with (label, yield, order) triples, we can extend the definition of the intersection tree as follows:

- The nonterminals of $T \cap T'$ are those (label, yield, order) triples that correspond to nonterminals of both T and T' and whose unary parents (if any) are also nonterminals of $T \cap T'$.

- A node n_1 is a descendent of a node if either $\mathrm{yield}(n_1) \subsetneq \mathrm{yield}(n_2)$ or if $\mathrm{yield}(n_1) = \mathrm{yield}(n_2) \wedge \mathrm{order}(n_1) \leq \mathrm{order}(n_2)$.

We can assign **induced dependencies** to a node given a suitable head assignment function as follows:

Given a head assignment function $\mathrm{headidx} : \Sigma \times \Sigma^* \to \mathbb{N}$ (such that $\mathrm{headidx}(p, c_1, \ldots, c_m) \in \{1, \ldots, m\}$) we can recursively assign a head to each node by using:

- $\mathrm{head}(n) = n$ for terminal nodes

- $\mathrm{head}(n) = \mathrm{head}(n_k)$ if n has label l_p and the children $n_1, \ldots, n_m$ have labels $l_1, \ldots, l_m$ and $\mathrm{headidx}(l_p; l_1, \ldots, l_m) = k$

The induced dependency graph then contains $\mathrm{Range}(Term)$ as nodes. For any pair of a node n and its child n', the dependency graph contains a dependency edge $(\mathrm{head}(n), \mathrm{head}(n'))$ as long as $\mathrm{head}(n) \neq \mathrm{head}(n')$.

Association for Computational Linguistics
209 N. Eighth Street
Stroudsburg, Pennsylvania 18360

ISBN 978-1-5108-2521-5